The Gasconade Review Presents:

No One Sees the Irony

Edited by Jason Ryberg

Spartan Press

OAC PRESS
OSAGE ARTS COMMUNITY

Spartan Press
Kansas City, MO
spartanpresskc@gmail.com

OAC Books
Belle, MO
www.osageac.org

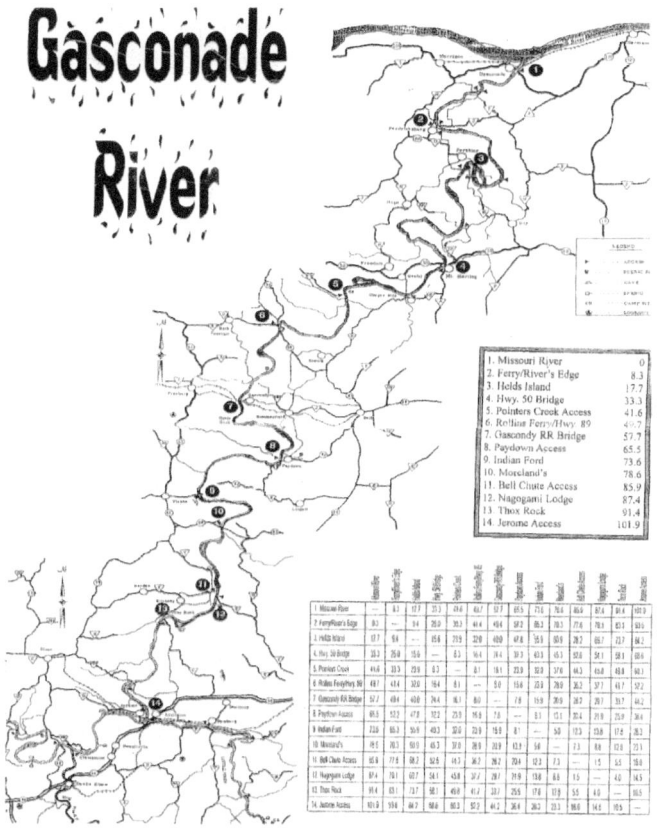

The **Gasconade River** is about 280 miles (450 km) long and is located in central and south-central Missouri in the United States. The Gasconade River begins in the Ozarks southeast of Hartville in Wright County and flows generally north-north-eastwardly through Wright, Laclede, Pulaski, Phelps, Maries, Osage and Gasconade counties, through portions of the Mark Twain National Forest. It flows into the Missouri River near the town of Gasconade in Gasconade County.

The name Gasconade is derived from "Gascon", an inhabitant of the French region of Gascony. The people of that province were noted for their boastfulness. It was applied by the early French to the Indians living on its banks who bragged about their exploits. The name means to boast or brag, and thus the river received its name. The waters of the river are boisterous and boastful and the name is also descriptive.

The headwaters of the Gasconade are in the southeastern corner of Webster County northeast of Seymour, Missouri where it drains the eastern margin of the Springfield Plateau at approximately 37°11'54"N 92°41'44"W. The river joins the Missouri River at the city of Gasconade at 38°40'28"N 91°32'55"W The river follows a meandering course through the Ordovician age dolostone and sandstone bedrock of the Ozark Salem Plateau creating spectacular bluffs and incised meanders along the way. Numerous springs and caves occur within the drainage area and along the river course. Significant tributaries include the Osage Fork of Webster and Laclede counties and Roubidoux Creek and Big Piney River of Texas and Pulaski counties. The Roubidoux and Big Piney flow respectively along the west and east boundaries of Fort Leonard Wood which lies a short distance south and east of the Gasconade.

The plateau surface near the midpoint is 300 feet (91 metres) above the river bottom near the river midpoint northeast of Waynesville creating scenic river bluffs. At the junction with the Missouri the river bottom is about 400 feet (120 m) lower in elevation than the old plateau surface above the river. The elevation of the plateau rim at the headwaters is at or above 1,600 feet (490 m) with local hilltops at over 1,700 feet (520 m) (second highest elevation in Missouri near Cedar Gap). The elevation at the confluence with the Missouri is 500 feet (150 m) giving an overall drainage basin relief of 1,200 feet (370 m).

It is ranked with a difficulty of I and II (seldom) by those who canoe, kayak and float. It is considered a good float stream because there's typically not a heavy congestion of boats. It is common to go for many miles without seeing another boat.

There are caves and an abundance of wildlife along the river and is considered a popular place by anglers for its largemouth bass and smallmouth bass.

The Gasconade River is the longest river completely within the boundary of Missouri. It has been called one of the world's crookedest rivers.

The *Gasconade Review* is a literary and arts publication based out of the Osage Arts Community (http://osageac.org/), located on the Gasconade River, just outside of Belle, Missouri. It appears twice annually, focusing primarily, but not exclusively, on writers and artists from the region and state, but occasionally also features *folks what ain't from around here.* All submissions must be hand delivered between the months of April and October and the hours of 3pm to 6pm. A decent bourbon is appreciated. Proper river attire required. Don't worry, the dogs won't bite.

TABLE OF CONTENTS

No One Sees the Irony

Timothy Tarkelly

Private Land

He left the gate unlocked.
A decrepit trailer sagged to the shape
of the ground, like a sunken ship
resting on a fertile floor.

A road reclaimed green
wrapped and unwound itself.
Out of sight, I unloaded and set foot
toward the dimness, forgotten acreage
weighed down by sweeping trees.

Bodies bemoan inertia.
Waterproof boots snag in the underbrush.

It was a wild stretched beyond recall,
a whole chunk of space outliving its own use.

No Kings

He torched the trees
And hoped to singe the sky

Anything to starve the soil
Make it groan his name

Crowns shine lauded over
Earth's dusty corpse

Taking is our first impulse
It lives in the lungs

Feeds every time
We cut our lips on his ring

Hawken

Mitchell lived the flintlock blues:
throbbing thumbs, wet powder, a pan
that couldn't muster simple chemistry
when the time came, its own heat
lost to gray mud.

The shifting wind sent the doe running
as far from his stink as possible.

It's all wet thermals and bad fortune out here,
a disappointment that stalks
any flash of breath, the frosty flare
of attentive blood.

There was a time when the mountains
were governed by such men,
sour spots in the snow,
the natural law of cast iron,
all parts doing their thing.

Mike Jurkovic

one of them

A certain suburban gonad twister and his scorpion maid
buy the house next door and there's no playing field
long enough   no playing field   wide enough
to escape his agitation: The mechanical slur
of his fictional lawn. His new rude machine
that cuts the land his imperial way.
He's one of those gear-heads
who rpm and revs you awake
each Saturday morn at 8am.
Hoards lawn jockeys and
talks to his tools.
Yea he's one of them
who I wouldn't have dreamed
to call one of them
that weekend   at Woodstock   Newport   Monterey

the other disciple whom Jesus loved

Peter, the Apostle, was an affable dude
who
denied
the boss
three times
and charged
headfirst
into the
churning
Galilee.
Who
wrote
this book
about
disquiet
y'see
its
tenterhooks
and daisies.
Its manifestations of pain breaking like thunder
from the
left shoulder
down
your
arm
into
your
chest
seizing

your
heart
w/
falsehood,
rumor,
and conniption.
Could you
give him
back his
book please? Tell him thanks for me.

Weird Left Eye

No one thought   I'd   amount to much
but   Mom   held out   hope   God bless her.

She saw something   in her   egg shaped kid
w/the   weird left eye that   everyone overlooked.

       I have   a way   w/ words
    that make   Mercenaries gather.
     Men vote.   Soldiers obey.
      Reams of rot   and slogans
    to hook   the kids
       into the   game

     I have   the boss's daughter
on her knees   and her twin next door
       doubling down

     I send the drones   I pretend
      to answer your prayer

Alexej Savreux

Eating Korean Pork & Kimchi & Rice at Christmas in the End Times

Slow-cooked pork with sodium-laden Gochujang sauce
White rice and ginger vegetable salad and dressings
Alcohols and Coca-Cola
Kimchi and avocado post-everything
There is no snow outside; there is not much snow anywhere
Some say the downfall of humanity, the world, and the times
A new dark ages;
Laughing, eating scrumptious food
Laughter is all that there ever was is or should, or could be
Stereo plays "New York, New York" by Sinatra
We are eating in New York at home for X-mas
And "Que Sera Sera" sing along, sing along
We laugh, we eat, and carry on and such
In the company, there is comfort and Love
The food is SO GOOD!
We stuff ourselves
Drinking beer like water
Playing darts and having all KINDS of parlays on the Chiefs,
Bills, and so on, $940 + on Mahomes and Allen!
Calm as can be and happier than happiest can be
The Christmas traditions continue uninterrupted
I got "Message," that Portuguese masterpiece for Christmas. It
    was a gift from Peter and Anna when they were in Lisbon or
    wherever; now they're hitched. Dope.
The Philly Specials with Jason and Travis Kelce
And Springsteen plays back to back on the stereo
At full blast: "Santa Claus is coming to TOWWWNNN!";

Armstrong sings "What a Wonderful World"

And my thoughts EXACTLY

And nostalgic, N-O-S-T-A-L-G-I-C! NOSTALGIC!

Photos of me as an 18-year-old, scraggly-haired, probably
about 210 lbs

Then the classic:

"I DID IT MYYYY WAYYYY!"

I swear to God, play that at my funeral many, many years
from now

The Sid Vicious version, like at the end of Goodfellas

Ah, what a grand life it is, indeed;

Some. Kinda. LIFE!!

Call me LiNgUiSt

And so, what makes me sad about machine learning and AI?
Is it the rapidly escalating global cold war and the AI arms race?
No, that's not TECHNICALLY new territory.
BUT what about the factually unsophisticated truth that we are
pouring billions into making machines more clever than humans
while we simultaneously defund public schools and communicate
via emojis and memes? While we become dumber, the machines
become smarter Well, then, I'm not an AI skeptic...literacy (not
just psycholinguistically) but LANGUAGE is so goddamn
existential. I am proud to wear the appellation "Poeta," but I am
grateful and humbled and ever so excited to be a scientist of the
word.

A Series of Japanese Techniques
to Make Life Better!

To discover one's purpose in life?
determine the reason you wake up each morning; choose
that which aligns with your strengths, embodies your values
and passions, and is something the world needs
Focus on minor improvements every day
nothing significant or major, just little things
Take breaks if you're stressed or being overly productive,
walk away, and then come back to it after a bit of a respite;
Eat until you're about 70-80% full (something that is said to
be a key to longevity)
What did they once say?
For we never repent of having eaten too little?
The beginner's mind is the Master's mind; therefore,
approach as a beginner in everything you do
And embrace imperfection! Perfection doesn't exist, and
done is, therefore (and likewise), far better than "perfect."
Spend time in nature for a good portion of the day. One
needs nature but does not need technology. I despise
technology. The Industrial Revolution and its consequences
have been a disaster for the human race
live within your means; frugality is ideal;

Richard Stimac

Alluvia

We are river dust,
undulating silt of sand, clay,
broken pieces of quartz.
Floods birth us. When the river
sloughs its lining and deposits
its burden across the American Bottom,
the river, potent mother, carries us
to term, saves us from cross-bedded
deltas, then dissolving salty seas.

Desire

You'd think something like a river is a fixed thing.
Maps, no matter how old, keep rivers in the same place.
Names change. Boundaries move, or dissolve.
Arrows mark migrations and invasions.
The river, given erosions and sediment, stays the course.

Like children, or cats, fixity is what adults desire.
All things change, with time. This is a truism.
But some things change so slowly, so easily unnoted,
we assume them permanent and build our imagination
    around them.
To think things can be otherwise is to be a god.

That was the first sin, in the Land Between the Rivers.
The Serpent implanted an image in Eve: "What if?"
Eden could be different than it was. Paradise lost with
    options.
Wisdom is knowing all that is need not be all there can be.
After the Fall, we could no longer accept we simply are.
    Like the river,

that once enclosed Paradise, and now slowly dies in its way
to the delta, we turn against ourselves. We are not enough.
Or so I feel. Like the river never rests in its mindless meander,
through my works, my days, wants and grasps, kisses,
    goodbyes,
I long to be a fixed thing, without movement, without will
    and thirst,

to be a standing body of water, a lake, a pond, a flippant backyard
   pool.
But that's not true. It's the sea I fear, the end of course, when all
   the sediment
collected over a continent dissolves into salt water. There the river
   ends.
The maps lose their contour. Far at sea, we lose our landmarks.
Lost, we drift, and lift our heads to the stars, secure in their heavens.

Geometry

We are the earth, platted and plotted, and allocated.
And the sea, the relentless, unconscious sea,
as we know, from department statistics and bureau reports,
these dark, wide, silent waves encroach and reclaim the
    land, reclaim us,
until all we thought solid, soaked with our sweat, buried
    with our dead,
our blood percolated to chthonic aquifers,
all that dissolves, and, behind it, allots
forests of grey trees and abandoned homes
hung on stilts, as if we could flee from the future.
We know this will happen.
This we cannot prevent.
In some ways, it should be solace,
that from the dust of the earth,
the silt of the river, we have come,
to the lightless bed of the sea, we will return.

Tyler Robert Sheldon

Reunion

Grandma sells her home. She's older and
forgetting. She moves to my hometown,
unpacks the couch, and later introduces
herself to my sister, very glad to
meet her, make new friends.

New Place

At the assisted living complex, so cheery
it could be a hip new hotel, my grandmother waits
by the front door for Dad and me to arrive.
I've been up since seven, she tells us, smiling
and bouncing a little from excitement. *I just
couldn't wait to see you. What would you like
to do?* We say *we'd love to hang out at your place,
Grandma,* and it's true—this apartment rings
with the familiar tone of her former home,
its '70s floral couch and china cabinet, the huge
round coffee table fit for all of Arthur's knights.

She has NPR on the radio when we all get there,
this cozy room with its happy yellow paint,
so like the old place, and Grandma turns up
the dimmer switch. Dad and I sit in rockers
that I've known since I was born, and before
she takes the couch, Grandma gives my shoulder
a squeeze. The sun climbs its way through
the wall-length window's blinds. Though it's
not the place we knew, it feels just as safe as home.

The Tv's Out

October 2023

and so Grandma and I sit
on the bomb-proof floral couch,
which we say will surely be here
after all that's left is the horizon
and the venerable cockroach,
and we listen to the radio. Across
the world, terrorists attack Israel.
The folks on NPR stay calm.
Nothing they can say will change
the state of things. I get up
to grab some ice cream from
the fridge, make up two bowls,
and bring it over. Grandma smiles,
spoons up a small bite. She says,
the cable guy won't be here until
next week. On the radio, gunfire.
In the black mirror of the sleeping
TV set, the two of us, arms across
each other's shoulders, listening.

Steve Brisendine

the better part of valor

so maybe it's not
            murder hot tonight

but I wouldn't go
pushing my luck
            or anyone's buttons;

never know who
might have a balky
air conditioner
            in a beater Pontiac

a short fuse after
            that sixth High Life

and no better place
to be for the next
            fifteen to twenty

Tense 1: Brung

v. Past tense of "bring"

Come on now, it makes sense 'n' you know it.
Ain't nobody ever been *stought* by a bee, or
said *I just closed my eyes and swought* after
       hittin' a home run for the Legion team.

Ain't nobody ever come out on a pretty March
day 'n' said *Spring has sprought*, neither.

I'll give you that somebody mighta *sought*
a song, but it ain't the same thing. That's just
so they know what to ask for when KSCB
opens up the request line or Doug Brewer's
       deejayin' a street dance somewhere.

Now *broughten*, that's just for old folks, like
maybe your grammaw from Oklahoma or that
one uncle who ain't left Greeley County for
       more'n' a week since 'fore you was born.

It ain't exactly right, but you gotta let some
       things slide. It's family.

Tenses 2: Drug

v. Past tense of "drag"

This'n's a good word for storytellin', by which
I mean you might be tellin' stories just a *little*
        bit, but there's always truth behind it.

I mean, we all seen it last Friday night when
Johnny drug three 'em Minneola boys with 'im
inta the end zone; wadn't no stoppin' 'im.

And I remember you tellin' everbody how
you drug 'at buck a mile back up from the
river bottom to your pickup, and I didn't say
nothin' even though I know there's a spot you
can drive to within a hunnert' yards o' where
        you shot 'im. That's still a fair way to go.

There's effort in this word. It puts in the *work*,
even if you're just sittin' in the pew on Sunday.
Everybody been there at some point, when
the preacher drug out the invitation through
all the verses of
        Just as I Am,

even the third verse nobody ever sings, until
somebody finally bit the bullet and went
down for a rededication, 'cause that's the
only way anybody'uz gonna beat the buffet
        line up at the Golden Derrick.

Beth Gulley

The Safe Blue Sky

So many years
since I walked out
on the balcony
and watched the bombing
of Ilopango.

Now I walk a quiet
neighborhood where
birds of all kinds
call out from the trees.
I lose myself
in the safe blue sky.

When I hear about you,
children in harm's way,
I hold open a space
in the future
where you also
might walk under
the safe blue sky
and forget.

Going Without (An Erasure)

He hallucinates.
Yes, all the time.
Gently
she advises
going without
the memory,
then moving it
to the morning.
He nods.
He does not see
a snake--
my mother.

Green Raw Flutter (A Found Poem)

When you feel
the green raw flutter,
don't let yourself get lost.
You have your language
and your body.
Figure out how
to make
the right sounds
together.
You have a better
 understanding
of the rhythm
once you are in it.
This is a bright spot.

Kevin Rabas

[deer, cougar -- great basin, nevada]   *for Sam*

The desert deer down, claw marks / along its belly, Sam
comes / to see what has been / done, and when he sees,
he does not run, / but walks like a monk does, / quiet,
like water, he retraces his paces, his footfalls / back to
the car, a pawprint / atop his boot print, five pads, / no
claws. / Sam cocks his gun. / The lioness watches / from
the treetops. Little wind.

[in cedar city]

Autumn (9) is small, my sister's kid, and we are hiking the
sidewalk snow and slush in Cedar City with her two older
brothers, while their Dad gets shoulder surgery in the hospital
on the hill. I say, "Ok, Autumn?" and she says, "Yes." "Your
feet wet?" "No." "Ok. Good." And we hike about a mile in the
white-gray mush, slush, and get burgers, then coffee (for me) so
I can keep up. At the lights, I walk last in our little line of ducks.
Autumn is slow, and does a kind of dance as she walks, her
hands often out or up, and doddles, and I have to say, "Come on,
Autumn. Keep up with your brothers. Traffic walks don't wait."

[cello elegy]

Ashley: I had two big decisions to make yesterday: to take a new job or keep playing my cello in the university orchestra. I chose work. Things will be so much easier with some money. Plus, it's just too much in the dorms, bowed notes through paper-thin walls, and the reply, a fist against the wall, "Shut up. This isn't a concert hall," and I hate those cramped little practice rooms in Brighton. So claustrophobic. Like I'm dying. In a coffin, crouched, laid out, dying. It'll be much quieter now, and I'll be able to eat at Spangles whenever I want. Next year, I'll even be able to drink.

Dawne Leiker

Street Singer

I try to walk past you
but stop when I hear you sing
of dust in the wind
of dust on Pete's fingers.
Your voice rough cut,
singing of curiosities.

Step down, street singer,
and stroll the streets,
grinning dog by your side,
frog hiding behind your feet.
I'll throw a dollar in your hat.
You can spend it on Marlboros
or whiskey or birdseed.

Then sing to me your true song.
Song of the Cretaceous Sea.
Song of napping in vast pastures.
Sing me the day Pete guessed
you were in that giant rock.
When he heard your ancient sea shanty.

And how he set chisel to your face
so that I could see you too.

Where the buffalo roamed

Where young calves try out new legs
and shaggy buffalo amble toward the fence line
of the government-owned pen,
display case for passing tourists.
Just across the road from his watchful eye

Eye of the monarch. Survivor, fused
to tons of limestone, roaring and snorting
in tones only the artist could hear.

Arrows are no threat to his heart of stone.
Guns cannot fell him now.
He is the king of the plains
where six million of his wooly brothers
once roamed before their slaughter.
Before mountains of carcasses lay
as far as the eye could see.

His brothers tasted the waters of Big Creek
before white men claimed it.
His sisters' sun-washed bones littered the tall grass
along the transcontinental railroad.

Who pays for his near extinction?
What is the bounty for his greatness?

The rock who would be king
surveys the hubris, his haunches tensed.
Surveys the passing cars. The curious strangers.
The sons and daughters of his death

Rock star

To Pete Felten

I wondered what he ate. What he drank.
If he slept.
I wondered if he was real.
He with the face of an ancient teenager
carved from a chunk of the Sun.
Framed in flannel and khaki.

All around, his creations looked on.
Bison, cats, and unyielding women
whose monolithic thighs and grim faces
stand stoic through all seasons.

His chisel found a path.
He wiped the stone dust with his rugged fingers.
The dust settled comfortably on his brow.
While he chiseled, his stories sparkled with punchlines and Pete-ness.

This was the man who found Amelia Earhart in a chunk of limestone.
Who touched his finger to rock and drew forth Eisenhower.
This was the man who discovered proud ghosts living in the dried-up
    Kansas sea.

This was the man who reminds us always to wonder.

Maryfances Wagner

Aunt Mary Reminisces About Nonna

Right now, I wish I had some of Miss Fishbaum's
matzo ball soup. Hers was the best even though
she smelled like sardines. I wouldn't mind having
some of Uncle Johnny's calamari either. It goes
so well with your father's vino and a nice salad
with artichokes and olives like Nonna made.
Nonna liked that soup too, but she said
Miss Fishbaum talked too much—always a story
about her ungrateful son, her husband's
gambling debts, or her gout. Nonna was a fine one
to talk. *Gimme a sip of your sodie,* she'd say then
glugged three gulps and set the glass down. *Still
some in there if you let the ice melt a little.* She did that
to all of us, but we never told her no. She liked
sips of your Uncle's vino too. Gave her a glow.
She'd drag out those fancy leather chips
she had a thousand of and start shuffling cards,
still feeling lucky from winning last week's
poker game with her girlfriends. She said they
only drank tea. Uh huh. Your Nonna confused us all.
One minute saying her rosary or reading from that little
prayer book she carried around and the next basking
under her sunlamp to tan for those poker nights.
Nonno always gave money away, and Nonna always
spent it. Once, Nonno interrupted her sunlamp basking,
goggles over her eyes, to ask her why each month
she kept the rent money he was supposed to receive
from his tenants and instead bought a new fur hat,

dyed her hair pink or splurged on a new ring instead
of it going in the bank. *Don't be silly, Frank,* she told him.
*That's how it works. I need it. You don't. Men don't
need as much as women do. That's the way it is.*

Found Poem While Waiting for Hamilton to Start

Kinky Boots should be good. Let's get tickets.
You take marshmallows and stick them on both sides
with toothpicks, and the microwave blows them up.
He was only 17 when it happened.
I think pirates are really hot.
I'm betting on the color of Gatorade and the coin toss.
Hashtag. How do you know that?
Who bought these tickets? I don't like history.
So, you want to sit there instead of getting wine?
All of us could use a good martini.
I'm having dinner for 47, and you're invited.
You do have to wear a sombrero.
José Compass. He said he didn't know you.
How do you know where you're going?
It's the new 50. Pendleton's a dud.
Can you go back from Kennedy?
My son hand feeds his hermit crab.
She looks so knock with curly red hair.
Stop leaning over the side. You're drooling
in that lady's hair below. Ooops.
Lights going out. Sit down.

Holly Keeps on Talking Through Detention

Well, here I am, and I'm gonna try not to talk
nonstop since that's the reason I'm here, but
you know me. Mostly, I can't help myself like
when Jeff Ball was nominated for homecoming
queen. That was big news. The principal's trying
to squash the nomination, but the ACLU said
Jeff had his rights like the time Darrell wore
that *Satan Rules* t-shirt, and the ACLU said
he had the right to any religion, but the good
chance of Jeff being homecoming queen will
start a *poo pah*. See, I remember that from
Cat's Cradle. Shows you I listen. Because I talk
doesn't mean I'm not a good student. Anyway,
the principal ought to clean out his own house.
Students talk about him driving Erica around
after school, and he ignores that his vice principal
is making the beast with two backs with the head
cheerleader. I remember that from *Othello* even
though I didn't like that play or Othello. We all
were saying that line. My mother said when she
was a student, nothing much ever happened.
The biggest news was someone pulling the fire
alarm, a sudden fight in the hall, or the day everyone
went outside for the solar eclipse and the school
president streaked nude across the parking lot.
My mother says even a perfect child can burn down
a house whatever that's supposed to mean.

William Trowbridge

Aboard the Autumn House
"Oats Express"

Confined in that aqua mini-bus, they seldom
feel their oats, much less sow wild ones. They feel
the urge to venture from their soured rooms
in the "home" some may have joked about. They'll
shop some mall or watch a matinee,
the air no longer tinged with Lysoled dread
or daily warbles for "Nurse,"or "Momma,"or maybe
a metronomic "Help me." They've forfeited
their cars and houses. Their favorite food and drink
disturb their bowels and don't taste right.
Their hips and memories are on the blink,
their spunk AWOL. But these riders stay polite
and sympathetic, smile instead of stew.
Live long enough, they'll save a seat for you.

APOLOGY FOR OLD WHITE GUYS

Yes, we're taking the rap for everything
from global warming to athlete's foot.
But even the aged Vandals had good joes.
Some must have found pillaging a crime,

not to mention raping and burning. Some
might have preferred to stay in their tents
and nap or entertain the grandkids.
What could they do to stop that punk

Gunderic and his joy boys? Maybe when they
reminisced, it wasn't about skewering babies
or sacking Rome. OK, we've got Trump,
Putin, et. al. But what about Jimmy Carter?

You wouldn't find him grabbing crotches
or bombing hospitals. Or Mel Brooks, still
giving the Bronx cheer on sanity's behalf
to facists old and new. And don't forget

Tony Bennett, his brain cells winking out,
but still knocking crowds blissfully dead,
leaving their hearts in San Francisco,
or steppin' out with his baby, Lady Gaga.

Next time you see one of us looking lost
as he dodders along the produce aisle,
give him your arm in that long procession
that takes us all toward Cemetey Hill.

TEACHING SHAKESPEARE
BACK THEN

There they are, at their desks again,
looking much as they did when
mini skirts and sideburns were in style.
There's Paul the Objectivist, repelled by
Hamlet's vacillation. And there she is, my
most devoted student, whose name

I can't remember, and Frank, the brightest,
in his Big Smiths and seed company hat.
"I love Porsches, too," blurted Doug,
when I asked if there were questions.
"It's Portia," I said, "P-o-r-t-i-a."
That's Linda, showing a honeyed thigh.

And, of course, Jasonn-with-two-n's,
the class asshole, who acted as if
we were there to study his postures.
It seems as if I got issued one of him
every other term. The others are also here,
gray center of the bell curve, whose faces

seem interchangeable. And there I am,
up front, groggy from grading papers
till one a.m., as I try to persuade a few
that Shakespeare isn't just for twits,
stuffed shirts, and English profs—before
Jasonn snags Linda's attention again.

But I had my days when things went right,
and I thank the hoary spires of Academe
for the dear, steadfast what's-her-name.

Gary Lechliter

Questions for a Ghost Town

What happened over the years
to pad the loss? Was it the railroad's
slow decay? Depots closed,
boxcars rusting on the tracks?

It's hard to pin down the truth.
When no one cares enough
to search the archives
for evidence of wind and ruin.

Where are the flowers that
once graced the city square,
the daffodils, roses, and periwinkles?
What became of the marble
statue of the local hero?

Why the boarded-up windows
of the five-and-dime store,
the cash register and soda fountain
where the locals gathered?

It's clear from what we know
that no one lives here anymore
except for the stray dogs and
cats, ragged and moonish.

Walking in Darkness

*It is the darkness that makes the light visible
and not the other way around.*—Nancy Venable Raine

I take our little dog out to stroll
through evidence of night rains
and the moon's illusion. Up ahead

the taillights of a UPS truck blink
to announce that a package is
wedged on our neighbor's doorstep.

All along the streets and driveways
holiday inflatables are out of sorts,
their hues timid and becoming absurd.

Where someone is walking to their car,
the remote starter turning the engine,
slumbered headlights popping on.

The Man in the Chimney

I often wonder why you tried
to shinny down the bricks
without so much as a friend
to save your life, stranded,
where no rope or safety harness
could haul you out alive.

Psychologically, it doesn't make sense.
And sense holds our better angels.
Sometimes we scorn what's right
for what should never be done
in a world reduceable to caveats,
laws, and common sense.

It isn't hard to imagine the hours
and days of futile pleas for someone
passing by to hear your muffled
cries, death's music, worn and
raspy, stuck in the groove.

Where you hung like veal unable
to scratch your nose or dry your eyes,
spiders crawling in and out,
sparrows perched on the bricks
to sing and nest, where angels,
small, glide in the bur oaks.

Linda M. Lewis

Coyote Crossing

She cast me a yellow stare--
the roadside coyote--
as my car passed
her statue-still pose.
Ahead she had loped
across the highway,
halted, turned,
stood her ground--
brush rigid, ears alert
and pointed skyward.
In the dappled shade
she stood brown-gray,
flecked and regal.
Self-assured. Brazen.
Glancing back I saw
two half-grown pups
bolt across the road
in my wake. The three
sprinted onto a meadow
of wildgrass sun-washed,
bleached and dried
to beige and amber--
an exact match to
autumn coyote fur.

They fanned out, sped
across the landscape
in a flowing triangle
swishing the brittle
grass that tickled
my pawpads as
I raced after.

Reading at Ad Astra coffeehouse

on a Sunday afternoon
when autumn stages her
final flamboyant display and
pumpkin-spice latte wafts
ambiance, I take the mike,
my back to the plate glass
window fronting Santa Fe,
command my vocal chords
to overpower the sputter
of coffeemaker and murmur
of caffeinated patrons when
half a hundred obstreperous
bikes cruise past on the Fe,
a testosterone-charged
parade of marauding hogs
who shout and sass and grumble,
rev and roar, threaten and fart,
grunt and belch and whine,
make no concession to an acolyte
of a quieter more subtle school.

Holding On

Only yesterday Autumn moved out, having
packed her satchel with warmth of sunlight,
carnival of color. Swish and snap of leaves
crisping underfoot. Firepit evenings of wine
and laughter on someone's congenial deck.

Now here's January, full of callous indifference.
Fiery blizzard alternates with abysmal fog;
numbing slush with freeze and sleet. A ghostly
snowbound world. Nobody rings my doorbell—
rare visits being bill delivery and the Culligan man.

Sidelined by blistering cold, I polish off a cocktail
of herbal tea and Ibuprofen, open Facebook
to find someone's post of tropical splendor,
await a Spring that may never breeze in, mope
about weather waterloo and global disaster.

Walter Bargen

Catching A Bullet

Deep in a deciduous forest
Some people would say hidden.
The election is a few weeks away.

In fall, oaks get pushy.
Never cut back, they grow
too close to the house.

Their acorns come knocking,
Ricocheting off the metal roof,
Sometimes wildly loud.

Thrashed by a rough gust,
It's closer to automatic gunfire.
With the front door open,

Welcoming the warmth of a fall sun
That slips in and curls once about the room.
A friend on the next road,

Who sold all his guns decades ago
Bought a pistol the other day.
His wife said they only need five bullets

And three are for the horses.
He told me I needed to buy
A 12-gauge pump-action shotgun.

He said the very sound of cocking
Is enough to scare off most intruders.
And once the trigger is pulled,

I won't need to worry
About my aim or worry about
Catching a bullet.

Facing the Music

The small fan clipped to the edge
of the wooden table,
where the cat bowl sits
mounded with brown pellets,
is playing Schubert's Requiem.

The washing machine
stuffed with pillowcases and panties,
draining for the spin cycle,
is singing an aria.
Even the blender has its rap
frothing frozen orange juice.

She's afraid to turn on the faucet,
afraid what more she might hear,
what confessions might flow forth
and fill the stained sink.
The crowns and filings in her teeth
are already tuned to the local
FM station. Another day of Faith Hill,
Tim McGraw, and a resurrected Bon Jovi.

*

Wriggling across the cut grass
near the clothesline, near the belly up
cat waiting to be stroked,
a score too long to be measured,

a signature beyond syncopation,
a staffless segmented locomotion,
a smashed-thumb-thick,
hand-long caterpillar,

something so out-of-this-world
so beyond a "B" rate sci-fi movie,
it would make Ed Wood proud,
the ten ballooning lime-green

segments encircled with black-punk
spikes bumping and grinding
as it crawls, head crowned by two rows
of three gaudy orange-tipped antenna,

a swept-back version of Mercury's
winged helmet, it's face a jazzed jumble
of colors, fronted by a bulbous nose
shiny as a train headlight.

The friend who's come to photograph
the larva stage of the Royal Walnut Moth,
says a thousand to ten thousand
invertebrates are lost each year,

perhaps a thousand vertebrates,
we just don't know,
we don't know how quick
to write the mass for extinction.

Dull Progress To Salvation

The woman with the crowning oak tree
tattooed in dendritic detail
on the back of her neck,

roots rising up from her shoulders,
moves between tables, brown t-shirt
and holey jeans, topping off

coffee cups, taking late-night orders.
The round back of her shaved head,
a blank billboard over a tangle

of stricken branches. Customers
intent on reading their cup-stained bottoms,
the prophetic limits of their late lives.

Above Formica-topped tables, steam licked
windows wait to evaporate into
clearer vistas. This ending looks closely

for what lies out there: streetscape, escape,
a tree on the back of a woman's neck
that must sometime drop its leaves.

Michael Poage

Old Town, L.a.

Yes, I know that, she said
While staring off into some
Scream coming from the planet
Called Venus. She felt compelled
To get there and find out why
The disturbance. She walked
Into Union Station here in L.A.'s
Old Town. I stood outside in
The fool's gold light of this
August near Chavez. I got
Worried having let her out of
My sight. In her manic
Mood she will spread her
Wings and dance with anyone
And her advantage would be gone.
So, find her I said, I know that, she said.

"Life Enrichment" Has Been Cancelled for Spring 2022

so keep a sharp eye on
the door. What kind of non-sense
comes to you as common sense?
For your Profile, hover over My Account
icon on the COP, click on Profile, copy
the URL from the page and paste below
before it all goes blank. You might
be required to provide a second
verification code, some numbers, or letters,
or identify the number of taxis in the photo
grid. Then click on 'I am not a robot' even
if it is not true. Without LIFE ENRICHMENT
being a robot will not affect your
Profile, who you think you are and the struggle
to find meaning in the URL. No matter what
keep a eye on the door.

Discretization techniques

i thought it was
a typo at first
a word I had
never seen but
sounds like the focal
name for some
inquisitional torture
turns out it is
a part of the
vocabulary of mathematics
not sure what it
means never knew
anything about
mathematics next
day no reason just
a quiet drain of
water or the blood
of your people
mixed with the ashes
of your village wherever
the location of such
techniques it will
always be discretization

Scott Silsbe

A Short Catalog of Delights That Made the Literary Festival Worth My Time

The woman, a stranger, who, upon seeing "Pittsburgh"
stitched in gold on my black hat, said to me, "Go Steelers."

When, over pizza & beer, Chandra heard the restaurant's TV
say that "National Tight Ends Day" was fast approaching
and she repeated it and laughed until she was red in the face.

Irwin's multiple prank phone calls to an Ohio congressman,
who he left voicemail messages for, affectionately addressing
the congressman, thanks to the Buzzcocks, as "Jim Jorgasm."

Or when Jenny asked Irwin what else she is supposed to
do for a living (besides teach the youth of America), and I,
being a smartass, suggested ventriloquism, and Jenny
seamlessly went into showing off her ventriloquism skills.

Or else the moment at the festival when Irwin asked me,
"When you're at one of these things, do you ever find yourself
wanting to just start randomly barking very loudly like a dog, sir?"

Wicca for Beginners

after Adam Zagajewski

Children come in off the streets, shuffle through the door.
They look freakish to me. But in a way that makes sense,
makes me feel like all is right with the world. Young and
bookish or artistic weirdos *should* look strange, I figure,
to men like me dangerously closing in on the age of fifty.
One of them approaches the counter and asks me meekly,
"Where's religion?" And how should I answer that one?
I think they mean what aisle they should wander down—
they seek direction. And I understand that kind of desire.
I consider a witty answer but point them down the aisle
with shelves labeled "Christianity" and "Eastern Studies."

I go about my business, researching a book on the shop's
computer to see if it holds any value, see what it's worth.
I look up and the one I directed is now standing there—
they have a book in hand and they set it on the counter
without a word. The book is called *Wicca for Beginners.*
"Three bucks," I say. And they pull out their coin-purse,
select some pieces of silver that amount to three dollars,
that'll lead to a kind of new understanding of the world.
"Bag?" I ask and they look into my eyes with longing.
I hold up a black bag. They look away and exit the store.

Orbital Perspective

Isn't it pretty? The neutron star collapsing, balancing
over the black ocean. And our dandelion fields full
of the strange cosmic beasts we like to give names to.
I couldn't stop looking at the shadow of us there—
it looked different after our difficult, lonely journey.
I, too, felt I was destined to join in a great experience.
It was freeing, in a way, to be so arrogant in my beliefs.
To lean in fully toward that kind of dimensional realism,
navigating the change and the changeless, the universal
and particular. A trash-truck woke me from dreaming.
I parted the blinds a bit and out my window, I noticed
the sky down in the gutter, a flowing atmospheric river.
Sometimes, but not all of the time, I can find the music.
I'm glad I could be here. I'm happy you're here with me.

Kevin Ridgeway

When My Mother Took Me
to See Lord of the Flies

Not Piggy! My mother had told me
to trust her smarts on her selection,
as she was in Mensa and therefore
genius enough to have read the book.
She said it was a friendly boyhood romp
set in an island locale, with
Goonies-style mischief to distract us
on a long afternoon of her paid vacation,
a second run showing at a dollar cinema.

I cried when the savage kids dropped
a boulder on my favorite character's head
and smashed his face in bloody murder,
my head turned away from the screen,
buried in the arms of my mother.

I felt her stomach move up and down
suddenly as I cried, and I realized she
was laughing, tears in her eyes. I still
have no clue what she thought was so funny.
Maybe it was a deep, dark Mensa secret,
her inner Beelzebub's rotten hieroglyphics
of the long history of her love for trickery.

She told me my IQ measured at 20 points
less than hers, so I presumed it was in
the dazed symbolism and a cruel language
I had yet to understand. Poor Piggy, alas,
my latest in a line of dead imaginary friends.
The voice of reason was silenced that day.

Low Blow

You look
just like
Eddie Munster
with your hair
parted and greased up
like that,
Peggy said to Jose,
who gnarled his lip
and winced.
A sustained,
dreaded *no*
came out
of his mouth
while everyone
else laughed
that's cold
he whispered
that's cold
and Pablo nodded
like an audience
member on Oprah,
without a clue
as to what was
even going on,
because he wasn't
paying attention
and usually does

that no matter
what anyone says,
including our
therapist, who
doesn't watch T.V.

Laugh, Love, Dance, Live(R)

I could not count
how many of the plaques
she had spread out across her walls,
nick-nacks who hid the unpainted grime
with something inspirational, the words
"Laugh, Love, Dance, Live"
painted on each,
which I saw in states
of grand inebriation
and scoffed at them as a wayward adult
living back at home with her
after a lack of marital success
due to an ongoing madness
that began in a dysfunctional home.
Those words were not advice
she took until the end of her life,
when she laughed in the face
of her doomed reality, comforted
by a grandson's extension
of her genetics no matter
what became of her. Years later,
my doctor informs me
I'm infected with Hepatitis C
and I walk out of the office,
tell a few friends in a lost daze
and intend to construct a plaque
for my wall that says
"Laugh, Love, Dance, Live(r)"
in honor of my mother's

stubborn reach for optimism
in the darkest clouds
of her existence,
her warped sense of humor
an infection she gave me
that I'll hang on my wall
to remind me to paint
my indomitable spirit over
all the shit that wants to kill me.

Nancy Krieg

mandolin miracles

Arthur Rubenstein practiced piano
on route to his next performance
the scores on his lap while on the
plane planning his moves like
the master he was

the fingers of my left hand
are numb but in my mind
I apply this technique
in hopes that my hand will
awaken and I will someday
play once more

the guitarist, Django Reinhardt,
burned his hand in a fire
his third and fourth fingers
useless except to dampen
the others zoomed around
the fretboard better than most
could ever imagine

there is pt
and squeezing clay
to strengthen my hand
though I wonder if
there is a chance..

before recordings

the first offering today
begins with a bass drum solo
two beaters pulsing a unique
syncopated rhythm the composer
born of at least four ethnicities
it's a native dance
the conductor's hair
punctuates the tempo
as she bounces the podium
jiggles

the symphony has great solos
but I'm searching for a theme
I can sing in my head
leftovers a la Beethoven
that repetition
he gifted
the audience
recalled as we filed
out of the concert hall

don't get me wrong
the reason I attend
is to hear all those
opulent viol strings
play in unison

I leave at intermission
the next piece roaming

in my mind
as I bounce
down the stairs
and escape
into a gorgeous day

poet's write

my English seems inadequate,
centuries of emasculated dissonance
logic, cured and crimped, jagged
edged puzzled parts, don't seem to fit
lyric style is all I hear,
I struggle to make art.

a musician can learn all the notes
of a song, though perfectly played
the sound that reaches ears
seems dull and flat
if sprung only from the mind
your soul may not speak,
but it knows the difference.

there are layers we build, haunting
archetypes moved from the past
rock steady sediments, foundations
we lay down
in vision's future eye,
bleeding colors of rainbow sky
some ardent drips of hues reside
hands and palms in finger paint,
the myth of heart, soul and mind
share a trio from inside,
all these elements of the poet's write.

Ken Gierke

Crossed Paths

Two mule deer stand on the shoulder
of the gravel road, wait for the third,
frozen in my path. I wait, patiently,
for it to decide I'm not going anywhere
until it's safely on its way, its disquiet
at my presence in contrast with the quiet of
this hybrid moment. Our paths crossed
one time, yet I am on my way to preserve
the memory of one whose life ended
at the end of this dusty Wyoming road,
just as I am determined to preserve
the life that stands before me.

Driving Off, Minor

Monk spars with Coltrane,
weaves around and through him.
They roll along amid lightning strikes
that illuminate the dark sky.
Mist rises from the road's surface
in this dusk of midafternoon on a gray April day
with light rain that is reflected, multiplied,
rises to join that mist from the tires of passing cars
before joining the sheen of the road's surface
in my headlights. The sky before me opens
to reveal a road not so dark and hazards
behind me. Monk's piano never off, minor
discordance trails off to better roads.

Impatient Spring

Warm morning light eases the transition
from melting snow to winter lawn.
Four robins skip across the turf,
pausing to peck at both soil and snow,
ignoring juncos and wrens
that forage for dropped seeds
below a feeder monopolized
by cardinal, titmouse, and chickadee.

I step outside for the morning paper,
greeted by the call of another robin
high in the white oak that towers
over the yard. Snow is still banked
beside the driveway, witness to shoveling
during last week's introduction to February.
Beside it and below the oak lies bare lawn.
The robin calls to me, as if to say
snow may fall again, but we are here,
and there is no stopping spring.

Beverly Cartwright

In the Middle of the Cotton Trees

It is awkward holding you this way,
        without sunlight,
without a clear trajectory

and to hear the bird's cry, its wing
        a perfect fit
for your leather glove.

I pull back your arm
        and line up your vision with the black bow
and the railroad tracks.

Neither of us on firm ground anymore,
        even here, in the middle
of the cotton trees.

So quiet and still
        moonlit teaspoons that match
the ground's pattern.

In Blueberries

He came back to the farm
the summer after high-school
working in blueberries every day.
A mythical job where a person's hands
take on the color of the night sky
and you can't scrub the dusk from
your fingertips, even when they idle
poised over a page, or a moonbeam
or a bead of sweat, or a stolen drop
of Old Spice.

He came back, even though he wasn't "blood"
to the uncle who paid him in damp dollar bills
that took two days to dry out, stretched flat
underneath the mattress, then hidden in a salvaged
legal envelope. Then hidden again in the crumbled
binding of the family bible. The bible that had
everyone's name, even his, in the same
fountain pen spidery ink.

Riding in the back of the pick-up truck
in the pre-dawn, he sat closer to the old
strawberry hands than he did to me.
He would smile at them and nod at the horizon
while he ate cold cornbread and country ham
that was more salt than anything else, more
like the taste of his mouth than anything else.

One Sunday, his real blood, a blond-haired
half brother came to visit, sitting in the front room
like a carefully placed obedience dog, waiting to
stand when the patriarch stood. Waiting for
an invitation to Sunday dinner and leaving
with nothing but a glass of iced tea.

"it was too hot to eat anyway" he told me later
as we held onto one another's waists and claimed
forever something that was more than blood.

Intact

After she came home from what would be one
of the last hospital stays, my mother moved
some of the furniture around in her living room
and then called me to see how I was doing, and
to see when I was planning to visit again.

Of course ideally, I would have known about the
week-end away in room 316, but she
liked to be independent, and she liked then,
to stand in the doorway for just a few moments
striking what would have been a casual pose,
if not for the white-knuckled grip on the door frame.

When I arrive home from Alexandria, after
a two-hour drive in my 1980 Toyota, without
air conditioning, or other passengers,
I am somewhat red and somewhat flustered,
standing in the doorway of a room that has shifted,
since I last saw it, and in front of my mother
who has shifted a little as well.

She has her nurse face on, the same one she wore when
she put her hand on my forehead to check for the truth.

I could never lie to that face. I tried once,
bringing her a handful of red roses
from the next-door neighbor's yard,
telling her they had all mysteriously fallen to the ground
somehow, landing petals intact

right next to our side of the chain link fence.
She wouldn't keep them. Instead, we had to walk next door
and I had to give back the roses
and I had to apologize, and I had to pledge
that I would never lie to her again.

So, it surprised me quite a lot that day
when I looked at the new furniture arrangement
and I looked at my mother, and I put my lips to
her forehead to check for the truth
and I realized we were both going to tell each other
a handful of delicate, white lies
that would somehow land intact,
just on the right side of our hearts.

Linzi Garcia

Backbone of America

train
hauls
hundreds
of bone
white
turbine
blades—
a spine
of potential
energy
slinking
across
America

Fill Up

He uninvited me
to his wedding.

It would be rude
if the woman he thought
he would marry,
was there.

She doesn't know
about me or us.

I sent a wedding gift—
a heart-shaped box
of the best chocolates, no
note, hoping she'd fill up
and not eat
so much of him.

At the Library with William S. Burroughs

On the corner of 7th & Kentucky,
I watch cars turn the wrong way
down the one-way from a cushy
perch in this glass box
library that lurches
over a busy Lawrence street.

Burroughs never stepped
foot in this library, the library
that swallowed his,
but I think he'd like
the view, talking shit,
giving tourists the bird.

Tony Brewer

Losing It

Doc says it won't hurt
but he is lying

He's not even a doctor
more like an archetype

& then I woke up
dirt in my throat
from the grave

He was right
This couldn't last

Everyone wants heroic measures
but it only hurts

in the memory
which is forever
we hope

Loving the job

My furnace guys jerk
each other around
friends longer than marriage
and they spar "like
an old couple" says Ron
I was thinking comedy duo routine
the artificial back-and-forth
of bickering without malice
requiring no setup
You know how this one goes:
old couple fighting
telling you it's normal
means they've lost the words for love
if they ever had them
Grown into the grade school
shoulder punch
Insults raining like tiny kisses
but an occasional peck on the cheek
Mom and Dad were like
nothing I'd ever laughed at
She hysterical in his
invisible stranglehold
while he bitched out her every move
Me in the belly of it
burning gently like a pilot light
That's how I relate to people
Are you serious or joking?
Did I buy a ticket to a show
or are we related?
Jokes aside they do good work
with one-year labor guarantee

Old Zippo

fuel spent
flicked and flicked again

no flame
but sparks
make a signal
in the night

How long until I quit
and ask for a light?

Bound up in every try
a maybe

Maybe this time

Jaron Vail

the future never comes

I'm tired of living
by our forefather's rules
tired of race relations
and the blind obedience
that comes with it
tired of religion
money hungry preachers
singing hymns on Sunday
in their tailormade suits
the crowd cheers
as they tighten their blindfolds
even tighter
almost to the point of their heads exploding
you can't go to the hood
without passing seven churches
down the street from the liquor store/grocery store/
neighborhood medic
when you hang a left at the crack house
God will be waiting there
arms open
so, they tell me
it's ok
righteousness comes in the morning
so, we wait
on the next Roosevelt
to quote the brilliant Langston Hughes
or wait
on the next Obama

yeah

that seems more appropriate for modern times

he'll come riding down the street in a driverless car

thumbs callused

from sending hashtags

shapeshifted

into policy briefs

and townhall speeches

I'm sick of it all

maybe tomorrow

when I'm sober enough

to mildly care about the future

I'll try to do something worthwhile

for my children

happiness is relative

I smoke a wood tipped
wine-soaked cigar
after a shot of whiskey
it's a cold winter night
the faint sound of coyotes in the distance
gathering
before their next meal
I put out the cigar
head back in the house
when the whiskey and the smoking
catches up with me
my daughter will come to the funeral
to pay tribute
my daughter
and my favorite stripper
if I'm lucky
the truth
I will tell my daughter on my deathbed
is overrated
there is nothing more valuable
than living your art
whatever that means to you
if your art be religion
let it be
prostitution, acting, stealing money on Wall Street
whatever it is
let it be
then
I'll disappear to some dive bar

in purgatory
as I wait on a righteous God to decide
if an honest drunkard
is fit to live amongst the heard
of his blind
copesetic
sheep

dogs like us

our aging dog
is slower than usual
his eyes glaze over
a bit more
day by day
when he walks
he quietly moans to himself
with each step
his tannish grey hair starts to fall
a bit faster
every now and then
he can channel the energy
and the ego
to jump on the bed
or play fetch
a mid-life crisis
of sorts
I see myself in the dog
I'm also at the age
where the monotony of suburban life
forces me
to wait until I muster enough ego
to do something brilliant
every now and then

Alex Gildzen

Circadian

this morning lark
on early walk
in the dark
hears a pair
of owls
hooting back & forth

I go home
to write a poem

we all hoot
in our own time

it's light now
& I drink coffee
while those owls
begin their slumber

Jazzville

fish Bruce paintd
on my shirt
leap in & out
of water not there
as Luca plays gypsy guitar

music
lets us swim
in streams
on maps
not yet drawn

Stung by a Bee
While Swimming

in early autumn
bees line
edge of pool
like salt
on rim of margarita

they are so languid
some fall
into the water
their flailing
making ripples
on a clear surface

I enter their domain
for morning swim
& in a forward stroke
my cuppd hand
catches one
& the blades
of its stinger
scissors my finger

supposedly
scent of its venom
smells like banana
but I jolt
without a sniff
& jump from pool

my pain is quick
but
I think of the bee
its guts gushing
into water

I wonder how long
its drowning will take
& if its stinging me
will bring
a faster end

my morning swim
which energizes me
turns into contemplation
of life & death

my finger hurts
but not enuf
to keep pen from paper

Caitlin Johnson

The Minion Contract

You promise not to steal from Satan,
his most prized possessions being
the bodies flailing & boiling
in the Lake of Misery.

You are, however, permitted to play
as you see fit
with the tortured souls residing
among the twisted trees of the forest
past the lake, where only brambles grow.

In order to maintain your position
as a Minion, you also promise
to enforce Satan's laws among
the citizenry of Hell.
This includes but is not limited
to enforcing standards of labor
in the quarry, intercepting
those trying to escape through the gates,
& dragging back into the hoary depths
for further punishment
anyone in violation of their own
contract terms.

Please sign below, verifying your name,
serial number, and your current section of Hell.

We wish you luck in your new position.
Yours, &c, &c, &c.

My Ghosts Keep Following Me

Where can you find me?
Oh, nowhere in particular—
just a dusty, unused room in Hell.
It's where I hide now.
Not that hiding helps;
somehow, they always find me.
I could be in the sunken places
around Satan's throne
or mucking my way through
the implacable swamps
near the river—
I'll never outrun them.
They travel so well.

For the Wolf

who endeavors to evade
the evil spirit chasing him
through the dark forest

who is frantic to find
a safe cave or nook
for hiding his own body

who searches and scrambles
only to find the thickets
trapping him

who never did know
that Hellhounds are real
but only in your head

R. Nikolas Macioci

Sleeping With A Nazi

He flops onto the bed beside his lover.
She turns to accommodate him. The sheen
of street light anoints her back, the contour
of her buttocks, her crotch luminous as an eye.
She looks into his blank face. Its emptiness
frightens her. His fatigue crests. His limbs
sprawl. This could be an underworld scene
from Chicago, 1925: rampant
criminal is calmed by kept girl, but
this is Germany where gas ovens
prevail over gin bottles and whiskey stills.

He begins to doze. She rides him awake,
wide open, deep in. He chastises her
for hovering like a whore, impaled
on her own satisfaction. His nerves wiggle
like minnows from feet to fingertips.
He rolls over, resumes sleep, the skin
on his back a broad darkness. She risks
resting against the hollow formed by
the valley of his spine. Her breasts,
unaccommodated, brush his flesh with hope.
Like a thief, she wraps an arm around him,
steals a cold caress. She watches
his shallow breathing, slides her hand over
his, heat transferred to her forgotten body.
Turning away, she lies on her back, stares
at the ceiling, assumes he dreams and in them
cannot wait to kill.

A Room On Earth For A Virgin In Winter

You taste his tongue, swallow between kisses.
His arms encircle you like a cure for solitude.

More than fifty years you have saved yourself
for this infinite rapture, shed shelter of religious

mysticism to lie with a man on enthralled sheets.
Light from a nearby lamppost washes over

your lost virtue and nakedness. You met James
in a bar, liked his voice, his easy invitation

to lay aside the frost of your life. Even though
you promised yourself you would never have sex

until marriage, ticking of each year's clock
finally punched a dent in stubborn resolution,

and you waded through scant reluctance
to a neighborhood tavern. You press your head

against his throat, wrap yourself around his heartbeat.
Is this the moment you should weep as he rises

from bed and leaves you with a sudden vacancy?
You hear shower water, pull the patchwork quilt

around your neck as if to hide his absence.
He leaves without a promise to return.

Lingering at a window, you watch his car disappear,
stare at the snowy street, ruined white turned to slush

under late-night wheel tracks.

Dissolving The Bond Of Marriage

After mom's divorce from my abusive dad,
we packed suitcases into the trunk of her 1953,
maroon Mercury and headed to Florida, our
destination, Ocala.

On the second day of our trip, we sped along
State Road 40 until we entered the main entrance
to East Silver Springs Boulevard. At a food kiosk,
we grabbed Coney Island hot dogs and Cokes,
bought tickets to ride the glass bottom boat on
Silver River. I was twelve years old, excited
as a school boy free from class. Dressed in shorts
and sandals, I was ready for adventure.

On the boat, we sat on wooden benches.
Everything about the boat seemed normal except
for the glass bottom. Our tour guide pointed out
vents we passed over, one of which suddenly
dropped to thirty feet. We glided atop schools
of multicolored fish, rainbows with fins, and
more vents that dropped off to breathtaking depths.
The water, sapphire blue, was clear as the glass itself.

After the ride, Mom drove to Sun Plaza Motel
where she paid for a room with two single beds.
That night, as I fell asleep, I thought I heard alligators
growl outside the window, or was it memory
of dad snarling, waving a gun around in midair,
threatening to shoot if we didn't surrender
to his captivity?

Chase Dimock

Confirmed Bachelors

The elderly lady next door doesn't want
to take any reminders with her to Florida
and she knows bachelors like me
always need half empty musk bottles
and unopened bags of tube socks.
But the greatest treasure, she carries over
is the milk crate full of records.

The sleeves exhale a stale waft
of mid-century modern cocktail parties:
Schlitz, Chesterfields, and entire tables
of food encased in stately gelatin molds.

She declares her love for Jim Nabors:
"such a deep, manly voice, nothing like
Gomer Pyle." As she listens for the roar
of his baritone, I remember him singing
"Back Home Again in Indiana" at the Indy 500
after he came out. "That's a gay man, That's
an out and proud gay man!" I yelled drunkenly
in the stands. My friend reminded me the Klan
is still active in many parts of the state.

"Oh, and Liberace, I used to gaze at the album,
his champagne diamonds twinkling in his eyes
as he tickled the keys." I wonder how he could
play with the weight of gaudy rings on his fingers;

sleight of hand on the mirrored piano, flamboyant
camouflage dazzling an audience only seeing
their own reflections against the fall board.

She hums the first few bars to *Mr. Sandman,*
cuts directly to the line where the ladies swoon
over Liberace's wavy hair. I twirl one of my own curls
wondering if I'm supposed to share in gentle humor.
But the gravity of her wrinkles, her eagerness
to give me her husband's clothes show she knows.
Even stars have predations, and these men were safe
for her to love. She has seen the 3 AM departures
of 21st century Sal Mineos and Cary Grants
from my apartment and knows,
I'll keep her record sealed.

A Checklist of Hernia Risk Factors

(as verified by the Mayo Clinic)

1. Being Male

As a man, I am eight times more likely to
develop a hernia, eight times more likely
to move boxes and carry large burdens
without seeking help, eight times more likely
to grunt from the guts, hoisting that weight
to show all the other men who are not there.

2. Being Older

Every day it bulges further,
like the sea of elastic waistband khaki shorts
at a Steely Dan concert. I tell Sal, my midlife
crisis will not be the lease on a Porsche,
but a Studebaker left half restored in the garage.
The crankshaft cannot turn over. The radiator
has a leak I cannot keep plugged.

3. Being White

According to 23 and Me, 75% of my DNA
crossed the Atlantic. Their puritan abdominal walls
strained and ripped as they pushed
the other 25% of me off the land,
that little knot of intestine bulging above
their pelvic bones, aching as the stagecoach
bumped over the rocks, ruts, and bodies in the road.

4. Family History
Saturday mornings, the men clenched their
diaphragms and crossed their legs as the
hernia mesh class action lawsuit commercial aired.
The diagrams of inflamed groins
made them feel stitches ripping from within
like the patch on the screen door
where the cat scratched through
and ran away.

5. Chronic Cough
In Sunday School, I was taught to say "bless you"
so the Holy Spirit did not escape when you coughed
or sneezed. Alone, with nobody to excuse the profanity
of my body, I stifled every cough and sneeze,
stuffed the violence of God threatening to leave
down deep into my bowels
where he pushes daily to escape.

6. Chronic Constipation
I've been holding in the Holy Spirit for three decades.

7. Pregnancy
Nobody wants to place their hand on my stomach
and feel the Holy Spirit kick.

8. Premature Birth and low Birth Weight
Terms I first saw on cigarette warning labels.
Tobacco executives toyed with the idea of
promoting defects as a benefit to tired mothers
wanting a quick and painless delivery.
I was two weeks late, evicted through

the forceps' hidden side door, and plump
as the Christmas goose Scrooge bought
to absolve himself of sin.

9. Previous Hernias or Hernia Repair
My hernia is a Whack A Mole game.
When I push it back in, I can feel it popping up
somewhere else, through a hole in the stomach
where back burner coffee dissolves a sleeping pill,
through a hole in the heart where too many photos
threaten to burst open the locket, or through
any corroded organ, worn from the weight of metaphor.

Sparky's Burger King

In Los Angeles, we tear our houses
to the ground every 30 years
rebuild, taller, glassier, sharper
faux exposed brick compensating
for the amnesia of history; the Tuscan
elegance of rustic columns and fountains
that live only on Olive Garden menus.

So, I understand, when Alzheimer's
tells her this isn't her neighborhood, just
a cognitive blur of static and stucco.
Though the few remaining ranch homes
still camp on the far range of her memory,
the newly built mid-sized mansions
swelling to the edges of their lots cast
a shadow too dark for memory to blossom.

But when we drive back from the hospital
she trusts my hand on the wheel
as if she knew years ago, when I asked
for world maps for my birthday, and always
knew where to pin the tail on the donkey,
that I would be her navigator
and always find the way home.

Rounding the final corner, I point out the Burger King:

Remember when we walked Sparky,
how he'd whine and pull on the leash

at the smell of cheap burgers,
prop up on two legs
try to charge at the glass door?

I see the clouds
of her eyes clear with her first knowing glance.

Did he ever get a burger?

No, but he got inside once

Poor Spark

Stroking her sweater like the fur of her long
gone dog, she tells me Sparky knew this corner
was his crossroads. When we loaded him in the truck,
he hid in the footwell at the stoplight. If we turned right,
he sprang up, thrust his head through the window
waiting to smell the pines of our cabin to the east.
If we turned left, it was the vet to the west
and he buried his head between my shoes.

I wonder if a tree shaped air freshener dangling
on the rearview mirror could have put Sparky at ease
when we turned left.

Next time I pick her up from the hospital, If I wore
a paper Burger King crown like a chauffeur's cap,
would she know I am delivering her home?

Someday, long after probate has divided her possessions
and the developers have bulldozed her house

and the Burger King to build a high rise,
I'll charge at the doors, fog the glass with baited breath
try to jam an old key into the retina scan.
Somewhere inside I will see her wingback chairs
a reflection of myself haloed with Hot Wheels
beneath her Christmas Tree, and onion rings
I can smell but not taste.

Steven Bridgens

Hobo Bob Dreams of Heaven

…entertaining angels unawares.~Evelyn Waugh

Sure, heaven will be swell. All the great parties catered.
The napkins: Irish linen, huge, and clean, for a change.

The Vatican's old silver is all laid out, spic and span,
squared away, just like in the Royal Navy.

There will be bunches of great bands, for sure, and
no one up here cares what happens backstage between sets.

The angels are fun at all these parties. They don't
talk back after a few cocktails like so many around
here. They are good listeners.

The dogs and cats have all had their shots. They sleep
indoors if they want, and eat whatever, from the
endless buffet we all share.

Surely the weather will be swell up there. No storms
or rains or dangerous turbulent anomalies in sight.

Maybe a gentle Spring rain occasionally but usually
blue skies as far as Taylor's pilot can see.

No need for cops, the army, or government because
the locals there wouldn't put up with all that, the way
the suckers, rubes, and marks do here.

It's hard to believe what is swallowed whole, holiday
wrapped and hogtied special everyday here in my neighborhood.

Hobo Bob Reports From Down By The Crick

Good news, boys and girls. Life and death abound here at the crick this morning. It's all part and parcel of that big package delivered fresh daily at every dawn's doorstep.

Gravity pulls this stream towards me from somewhere up near that time-rounded ridge upstream. It runs down through here over layers of flat rocks, stacked as if on purpose.

It meanders past me now, splashing over the stones in my pathway. Here and there are strong young frogs, a few still tad-polish, happy to be alive, hoping and cavorting, always underfoot. Unknowingly, they await their fate, and like me, seek refuge here beneath the shade trees.

The current of the rock-bottomed creek is strong, and flows quickly by. Its width, depth and wavelength are dependent on a very complex calculus of climate and weather, time itself, and, of course, the planets above, spinning round and round.

The cold water eddies past my unsteady legs. Broken limbs and tree trunks have been forced up onto the banks during seasonal flooding.

The current pushed, pulled and scattered them every which way, but only as far as gravity will allow.

Continuing on downstream, I discover a rib bone and a hard carapace bleached by the seasons, now all that remain of small, former neighbors intertwined with me in this web of life.

They're left behind, in confused profusion and I've included
them with my extensive notes, along with untainted evidence
from the scene.

I describe it all here and report my findings to you,
otherwise engaged elsewhere.

Hobo Bob Contemplates His Own Mortality

The nights, the days, the dark, the light. Ho hum.
It's life and life only, as Bobby D. sang so lyrically,
once upon a long, long time.

The dream unfolds, the bubbles burst. The slender
moments rattle and gong like bamboo stalks on
ancient Chinese scrolls.

At dawn a skeptical old bullfrog glares up at me
from just beneath the empty mirror of a simple pickle bucket
pond we share. He shows no fear.

But then again, no one is afraid of white men, when
first they meet. But just you wait, Froggy Gremlin.

We come as friends, bearing many gifts, stuff you don't
have and might not have, after we leave.

All in all, the only ones who will finally win are the
deathwatch beetles and, of course, *the conqueror worm*.

Yeah, I suppose the shiny green-backed scarabs
will get a piece of that big pie, too.

Somber dark birds circle above us now, just waiting
for a place to land.

L. Dopa

Sleeping in a Field of Unmarked Graves

I rode the wild river that runs through all our veins in order
to escape from the super-max detention center of the calendar
(each bare cell with its own merciless and indestructible clock).
I slept in a field of unmarked graves, where acres of bones
called out to me in my fitful dreams, filling them with strange
visions of a woman clothed in butterflies, a tree with antlers
for branches, a burning piano upon a hill, and all the while,
the moon stood at a respectful distance, but still more than
close enough for him (her? them?) to see and hear everything
I did or said.

Night Forest

You heard whispers
dreaming the night forest,

the strange fruits, the moon,
a mountain, summer leaves above,
the tall trees from long ago,
the birds hatching, a snake
slithering under her feet-

the sad woman, sleeping,
dreaming the hot watery dark.

Music and Thunderstorms

Random notes from a
wind chime hanging from a branch
is easy enough

to mistake for the
tentative beginnings of
a symphony as

a few drops of rain
are for a thunderstorm-
each drop part of a

continuum of hushed explosions,
each note a measure of wind.

Al Ortolani

Transistor Radio

My junior high band teacher
said my trumpet was a good instrument
even with the dents and the scabbed
alligator case, too good for where
I sat near last chair, hidden behind
the wooden music stand, next
to the window to the playground.
Once, during a sudden electrical storm,
a bolt of lightning shot into the band room
and nearly took our teacher's head.
The brass blew B flats, drums clattered.
One girl dropped her clarinet. Shut
the windows, the teacher said.

I left mine open a crack, suddenly
claustrophobic, the cool air
of the storm a tonic. My father
hired a private tutor for me,
and I walked each Thursday to a house
on Elm Street, a house well-sealed,
with rote scales and valve oil.
There were storms that season,
low heavy clouds, rain drops
on the alligator case. On our all-brass
challenge day, I told the teacher
I'd forgotten my trumpet. I dropped
to last chair, back behind the kid
who smelled like liver and onions.

In high school, my father had been a stand-in
for the Long Island Symphony, attempted
a thin moustache like Harry James.
My mother had slapped a bass fiddle
and jammed with a college jazz band.
She hung out with guys
named Binx and Fat Arlo.
She said I was tone deaf.
My father said he was wasting
three dollars a week on lessons.
At night, I tuned my transistor radio
to WHB in Kansas City, buried it
between the pillow and my dead ear.

Climbing the Tower at the Drive-In Theater

It was a long way to the top,
the wooden ladder nailed inside
the tower, two by four rungs still tight,
still defying gravity. I followed
you up, not because you were my boss,
the soon to be projectionist,
but for the adrenaline of a climb
so steep I'd pitch over backwards.
I climbed above the expanse of farmland
spread in a grid of hedgerows,
above the lives tucked into small houses
below mercury lights, above
the semi-circles of cars facing the screen,
speakers hanging inside windows,
windshields dark like sun-glassed eyes.
We toed as near the edge as we could brave.
Hollywood played across the screen, a flickering
dream of John Wayne, of Maureen O'Hara.
No one can see us, you said, our silhouette
lost in the night above the projectionist's beam,
shifting, rolling with each change of scene,
a magic act lit by a carbon filament
by a man in a small room through a small window,
film cannisters stacked along the wall,
whiskey bottles ratted behind the shelves,
behind the coffee cans of nuts and bolts
and spent carbon. A hundred feet below
sat the ticket booth in the driveway. A girl
I knew I could love perched on a stool,

taking cash, handing tickets to the manager,
who in turn passed them through the window
of a Chrysler or a Buick. I couldn't tell.
Soon I'd relieve him, sit with this girl
I could fall for. We signed our names
on the wall with pencil, concave on the mortar
between the bricks, where we assumed
they'd last beyond our time, beyond
the few hours we had, like the movie
below the tower I'd climbed, the two of us
where no one could see
our nervous hands, our fear of love
when the credits played, when at two a.m.
the last Chevy rolled out of the gate.

Stacking Dishes at the Lipstick Hotel

The head dishwasher smoked like a kid with a plan,
flicking ashes, picking tobacco
off his tongue, explaining
his next best job, how this
was nothing
compared to selling cars.

In the evening, after the kitchen closed,
we were left alone with supper's
stock pots and room service trays.
We played a game with coffee cups,
pictured the women
who left lipstick
on the cups.
We judged
the color, the full lips.
We took liberties,
imagined one of them the call girl
rumored on the 5th floor.

We kept the water hot, scalding, wore
rubber gloves, scrubbed fast
with nylon bristles, polished
with steel wool. With the sink empty,
we cleaned the drain trap, smacked free
the beans and pork, the gristle into the trash.
We dried, stacked pots,
dishes, tumblers, coffee carafes.

Tomorrow needed a start fresh.
The cooks
arrived before the sun, maybe
as the call girl was closing her door.
I owned a motorcycle.
Home in minutes. Studied algebra
to stay clear of Vietnam.

The head dishwasher waited

for the police to pick him up. He was
witness to something protected.
Some nights I waited with him.
He snuffed his cigarettes

in a coffee can, kept
his eye on the corner, the neon
Open
above the bar. He never talked
about the names he could name.
I could stack dishes, keep
my mouth shut. Happy
with a motorcycle that went
nowhere special.

Pilar Graham

Parade

This air movement is not simply a bodily reflex
of Lazarus, or artfully plastered at the top of any outer

rim, where Yama perches at the edge in all four directions.
These are part rituals, scholarly inhalations or illuminations,

where the order of instance becomes designed for the living,
creations of categorial monks who live on constructed grids,

when really… all subjects will find a way to settle into fine powder,
and breath will work last, making an exceptional interlace of itself,

becoming part of the natural, until the buffalo of-the-unforgotten,
adheres itself, next body's side, propping itself, after having fallen

in love from all the spectacles once afloat—electric pulses, where
life excelled with magnetic-colored displays, short surged, but you
    still allow

it to pass through you, though knowing it has already become
moderately obstructed, held by a half-staff, physical reminders
    of life, by way of death.

Attraction and Departures

We may never know
which end of the pole
we had been holding, whether
        it had been, north or south,
while at another entrance
to one another,

as we stood, as so many times before,
allowing ourselves to attract,
        using a way to connect,
playing with two magnetic blocks,
as our arms moved back and forth,
a soundless invitation of sorts of how

our bodies moved closer
with each push and pull, until
        we found rest in retraction
from the weight of day, gravitating
into dusk ... still, it remains
truth and loss cannot ever separate

between this pull in two directions,
even more so, when the evening
        falls blue, becomes motionless,
where wordless wind cannot be convinced
air messages cease to live in our departures,
while the neck of a blue heron stretches,
with you... now, outside my front door.

Winter Butterfly

It is because of you   I started
to pay attention   for the first time
to the forewings of flight,

to the delicate...
life of butterflies, or how
dialogue has a way to flutter

using four wings, and live between words, as if
repetition *is part* of making something last—
like words spoken last summer,

when new winds had arrived—
a bit like love—when there was an infinite   undoing,
like an achromic insect in the art of   becoming,

not yet flying, but shifting its body into   an offering of Light.
Yet, now   in our imago state, with wing spans
in all of its opulence and refraction of colored patterns,

we merely resemble two headdresses
of our silence, of our sacred nuns, and resist
our desires to taste the overripe fruit

in belief, we've already risen,
becoming   too spiritual for nectar.
Now, inside my house, you say, *Coral Reefs,*

a book tucked into a shelf, and I know
this is the same category in life:
For Viewing Only: we resist the inclination to touch.

I've become part of an aquatic paper underworld,
a mystery, where the confusion of currents
can whip flight patterns, not free from any risk,

as if a secular breeze   between   us
could shoulder our destiny,
as with the weight of knowing

anything, or how it has the ability
to wash away un-earthly spectrums
below the surface, and into old-aged regrets.

Yet, tonight, when you arrived
and wouldn't let me   break away
from the deep embrace of your span,

dissolving the post-misery of being grounded,
where the seasonal silence had stopped,
took note, and failed to stand still, since

as with any winter butterfly,
I flew aimlessly towards the pulses
of your lattice-wired heart and past the dreamscapes

of the Sierra mountains that seemingly pressed
their linear, and layered bodies of time, against
my back—and so, I leaned in deeper, since newly-emerged
butterflies are not expected to fly, and thought I heard the

ocean in the white stripes of your winged-breath.
It's starting all over, again.   Post-seasonal flight:

having *and* releasing. Let's repeat the present
tense   moments in the type of   nearly- knowing
love never knows when, or how,   to even stop.

Nettie Zan

Walking on Easy Street

listen
the man already knows
how to pick up the bones
and who to give them to
to make something beautiful
he's broken and fixed the factory
that blue-collar gristmill
and also pulled
the survivors from the line

listen
he mends our frayed lives
he tends the wounds and the light
and he tells it like it is
while feeding you dad crackers
chain smoking bargain basement squares
and standing up for all the down trodden

he doesn't lay down
in his fold-out cot
when he's tired
he watches over the sleeping
and when we wake
he's right there
with the black drip
the warm ride home
another pre-roll
a laugh that travels light years
he gives you hope

with every word he speaks
all torn from his heart
on his sleeve

listen
he's about to read a poem

Women in Poetry

are tough as termites
and soft as shoulders to cry on

they grit their teeth
and wring their hands
and have guns under the pillow
because they know
what their lovers are capable of
and they love them anyway

and if that's a problem
it's your problem

because the women of poetry
love harder than blood stains
fuck wilder than black widows
and aren't afraid to tell the truth
to you, the world, the children, all

they are the creator god speaking
a new universe into existence

the women of poetry
carry their own weight
and yours
sometimes
too

anytime

you need a hand

The Poem is Never About What
The Poem is About

your poems
are stubbed out cigarettes
with a guilty conscience
and a hopeful smile

my poems
are new buds on bare trees
that prove life springs
from death

your poems
are road miles and phone calls
that connect the heart
to the horizon

my poems
are running naked into the forest
and falling asleep in the arms
of water snakes

your poems
pave the streets with broken glass
and work eighty-hour weeks
to keep the water on

my poems
throw themselves down the river
without noticing there is no
way home

we're just the same
--singing what we know--
making prayers out of what is close

raising our voices against the wind

Sharon SingingMoon

Unbounded

The forest holds no secrets
life and death embrace
the damaged and the new
lie together, symbiotic lovers

No betrayal exists in the forest
you know just where you stand
on a well-trod path near the bramble,
or on a bed of leaves silently becoming soil

Under the safety of cloistered cedars
that celebrate both sun and moon
you may kneel, give up your confession
surrender to scents, soil, and silence

In the forest, trees dance with a breeze
delight in knowing their young
entwined roots commune beneath the surface
they do not weep to hear your sad song

No secrets remain in the forest
life and death sit close
worms and beetles and fungi
live their lives in innocent service

Stream and stones caress unbounded
the trees will not hold fast your troubles
but send them up and away
in the forest, you know just where you stand

Unrestrained Indulgences on Splice Creek

Spring shakes frogs into a sexual frenzy
peeps & groans bounce across stone ledges
bubble up from muddy banks
unrestrained indulgences
vibrate mucky puddles
Breezes carry love potions across
the creek into the woods
trees & bushes blossom
enticing pollinators with their sensual swaying
trills & tweets tell of returning birds seeking mates
they squabble with the permanent residents
vie for snacks & space

A committee of buzzards hovers
eyeing something dead near the road
a stand of daffodils recalls a homestead
now abandoned
an ancient apple tree spreads its scented canopy
over a partial foundation
buried by curly dock & dandelions
rain & sun conspire & overnight
fungi appear dancing across rotting boards
the remains of a home
a murder of crows discusses last
years' corn field, plotting
the moaning of a neighbor's calving heifer
floats across the low-water bridge
I walk the creek in wonder
witnessing this wild business of living,
I know the freedom of being inconsequential

Not Even the Dead

A boy, face smudged with grime, carries a scrawny kitten
his sister and their cousin struggle to keep up
make-shift crutches pinch their arms
as they practice walking with just one leg each

"A bit of happiness" was discovered in the rubble
they hand the forlorn-looking feline to a smiling
mother "what a blessing" she cries aloud
"another mouth to feed" she silently considers

The constant buzz of drones invades sleep, bombs drop
without reason there is no place to hide - she makes tea
with only water and a bit of lemon peel found yesterday
this must suffice as their evening meal

Across the hill bulldozers defile graves, toss shrouded
bodies into piles, demolish stone markers, smooth
the ground, erect walls for a military encampment
here in this hell, not even the dead will find peace

Julianne King

no one sees the irony.

if you live to be 100 or so
and crank out babies before graduation
you can grab a photo of 5 generations
maybe end up in the paper
cracked and crinkled hands cuddling rotund baby thighs
two women scowling
A young mother enamored, smiles
the oldest mother too near heaven to care about who else might
    care if she's going
the ones in between forced to carry the burdens
pay the extra groceries
pay the time in daycare
pay for the disapproving eyes scorn weighted dumbbells strung
across strong shoulders carrying water buckets full of shame and
unshed tears

this has happened twice in my family
we proudly display our five-generation photos
both of them
and hide the teenage mothers

both of them
no one sees the irony

if you live inside a body
born without enough or too much of the chemicals needed
to spark the machine to life
you can end up with a genius

IQ in the stratosphere
journals filled to bursting with inventions
four generations drowning
forced to carry the burdens
pay the hospital bills
pay for the pills
pay for the disapproving eyes scorn weighted dumbbells strung
across strong shoulders carrying water buckets full of psych
wards and slow suicides

this has happened twice in my family
we proudly display our IQ scores
all of them
and hide the teenage mothers' time in padded hallways

both of them
no one sees the irony

labels.

when I was 4 and wanted desperately to know
how everything worked
no one mocked me
instead bought me my first
encyclopedia
treasured my sparkling eyes and sponge like mind
and later when I wanted to know the whys
of the world
my father brought me a timeline of everything
stacked atop all the others
Egypt and Rome
Anne Frank and Aristotle
The Inca and a fledgling America
all together on a page
one leading to the other to the next from the other
spontaneously together
brutally apart

Why then
when I turn the query inward
seek just the right word for the me that is I
am I greeted with such
Malice
such Disgust
"Why must there be a term for everything" from those who
taught me words were the keys to every thing
scorn at my inquisition from those proud of my inquisitiveness
my nature did not dissolve as I grew
did not dilute as I stretched into this shape
I am still me

perhaps it is the way words have always held a power over me
pulled me into Grand parlors
forced focus on Haversham's aged hands,
urged me to follow creatures through forests,
tossed me down snowy hills with Jonas
scoured and revealed me.
words on pages felt real to me
I want to feel real to me

as real as the steam engine I have never seen
Jupiter's storm
Magma and electrons
I want to *feel* like all the parts are adding up to a whole
like the whole isn't broken from a sin I never committed
like whole isn't easily discarded
like whole belongs and has a purpose
like my purpose is more than just *not dying*
like I get to live and write it

and name it

cowards.

our goodness can be measured
in the safety others feel
in our presence
in the protection offered
to the most vulnerable
at their weakest

cowardice
is an unforgivable sin
indifference his carefully constructed
no longer accepted
excused

you only knew me as a child
i was only ever your child
you should have been my shelter
should have stood up to the monsters
your indifference was paid for
in scars and blood

my blood

it's not enough to
never lay hands.

Matthew Porubsky

from *The Kansas Voice*

What you hear is not flat or sparse.

Windswept. Stretching. Thoughtful. Even
throughout – rising as much as falling.

Bare as much as bountiful, this balanced scale
of scenery rolling beneath sifting hues

of morning and midnight luminescence.
Level as a filling sea – waves swell and cup, creep,

draw back on themselves, constant in occupancy.
Below water or vacant of, I spread the same as ages.

A variant pulse of veins.

      A subtle hum of rivers and creeks
      tumbling soft as last remnants of my past body.

      The surging squeal of the great steel railroad –
      horizontal god embellishing curves, twists,

      lifts, and openness of my palate of land
      to taste motion, eminence of circulation,

            tied pieces in balance.

Level.

> Vertical tumbles of grain elevators rise up
> across the scene as rural skyscrapers,
>
> concrete and aluminum pillars, churning,
> turning each year's yields. Intervallic
>
> cities between fields of variant heights –
> stalks, branches, mortared bricks, marble-casted,
>
> haystacks like hills, cut, dried, raked, baled,
> one great copper dome, portal eyes
>
> open to every direction, in turn viewing
> all the angles in working, lasting union.

Lynne Jensen Lampe

Empty Sleeves at the Patriot Store

A woman wheels into the VA clinic
for a blood draw, waits in a line five deep.
One vet asks the way to OT. Another points

upstairs with half a palm and two fingers.
A man hitches his hip, drags a leg
without bend. Halls full of people

broken. Summer rains soften
hillsides, water poppies in glass
caskets, each blot of red petals marking

investment with no certain return. The Patriot
Store hoodies declare *one life, one country.*
At dawn you nurse a hot cup of gunpowder

green tea and I pick blackberries.
A fledgling stares from the brambles.
Night thins to heron and geese flying

across a saffron sky, their gunmetal
gray stitching the dawn. A last shooting
star plummets behind the trees.

Duty scrapes cataracts from the eye
of a storm someone calls freedom.

The Day I Answer Your Good-bye

What thou lovest well remains,
the rest is dross.—Ezra Pound, Canto LXXXI

You fill a tub in your kitchen with water. I throw
off my t-shirt, unbutton my jeans, sit in suds.
You wash my back. Grab a beer from the door
of the fridge, tuck a pinch of Skoal in your cheek.
Ask about my drive. Were the redbuds pinking
Kansas? Was the double-hump camel grazing the east
side of I-70? How many rainbows? I reply *yes, yes.*
At least six. You quote Pound just to say the word
dross, a word you taught me a decade before.

I was so casual with my body then.

The box fan blows suds, the blossoms floating
a midnight breeze in the park the night we did
not spread a blanket. Our bare backs welcomed wet
grass, witches burrs, and the settled fury of petals.

Coil of Catastrophe

I chop carrots to the tick
of *60 Minutes*, most words a jumble
while I think

of food.
Despite the kitchen hum I hear
explosion in Ohio, mass shooting in Michigan, boy dead in Memphis—

TV words slide over, under, a ball
of snakes writhing
on the flowering quince outside
my window. Anger
knots my stomach, desire
to be right twists

thought. On a single bone-bare
branch, fifty males ribbon
their way
to a female, skein so tightly the pressure
suffocates
those most anxious

to mate. Yet they frenzy
21 days,
can't tear themselves away, won't reject
this coil
of catastrophe,
their own

24-hour news cycle.
The female knows stress
kills
and slips away
after a couple days
to look for food. I yell at Lesley Stahl,
still cooking.

Lesley Day

Manifesting Dreams

Dreams written in ink upon leaves,
ceremoniously burned to ashes
within a single flame,
caught by the midnight wind
and carried away
to lay upon the land of our ancestors.

Will the magic in this ritual
bring something more in the year to come,
than the empty bottles of hopes
that sat upon rickety shelves
before shattering at my feet,
of a year wasted away by sorrows?

Change in Perspective

I sat and watched my life,
Waste away down a dirty drain.
When I reached down,
And dug the life back out,
The perspective had completely changed.
It no longer showed the same definitude,
Of what is right,
And what is wrong.
I cannot lie,
I tend to like,
Its new and warped demeanor.
It's free from the common constriction
That used to hold me tight.
The things my mind once construed as fact,
Have faded from my sight.
For life is utterly fragile,
Even when we do the things
We once considered right.

The Lucky

The lucky will take
their weathered, calloused,
bloody beaten hands,
used to block the blows,
fight through life,
and wrap their fingers
around a memory of innocence,
clutching tightly to the
imagination of a child,
holding it close always,
letting it filter their soul.

They're the ones who fertilize
that bullshit life,
sprout buds that punch their fists
through the hardened earth,
and bloom into magnificent colors,
turning that bullshit
into some kind of beautiful.
Yeah,
the lucky ones do that.

Gabriel Ricard

$150 in Cash on Hand

No one found any cursed dolls,
or notebooks with a fast-track to the sort of Hell
that's just hung upside down with your head stuck in concrete
for all eternity,
or even proof that ghosts prefer microwave tea
and still suffer from Jim Henson's Cat Allergy Babies
even in the afterlife.

It was just a particularly hot day
to clear out the dead man's apartment
and not think about how or why or when he died,
or the nature of the universe,
or loneliness,
or why a simple stack of raving madman letters
can feel so utterly and gleefully cursed.

We finished loading up the truck close to sunset,
no kidding,
and we smoked cigarettes over a full bottle of coconut rum
that someone had found.

And then we talked about dropping the truck off
in time to go back out
and look for trouble.

Just another summer under the 1993 red sky.
Of course it was.

Room at the Top, February 2009

Dust yourself off, old, lumpy bean,
and try not to imagine what might be
coming down at a natural pace
from the supernatural potential of the rafters.

Even during the Civil War,
the first one,
this was probably an old train station
that no one would probably ever tear down.

You can't abandon history. Even if it is
at the edge of town,
but not so far that you couldn't build
a few apartment buildings that someone someday
will need to imply is a heartbeat away
from the Downtown Mall.

You don't abandon children.
You don't abandon smug, unreal alcoholics.
You don't abandon The Beatles.
You don't abandon typewriters,
the threat of walking up the wrong flight of stairs,
flea markets touched by the endless heatwaves,
fried eggs, Hogan's Heroes, Virginia Woolf,
or the same three arguments each and every day.

You go to work. You hope someone will mow
the grass in the theater parking lot. You project.
Project again. Drink the larger bottle of wine by accident.

Resent the potential hypocrisy
of a man with a room at the top of the world tonight.

Who isn't you. That son of a bitch.

You daydream about having over a thousand dollars in the bank.

You keep busy with community theater.
Tonight would be a good example.

You display your guitar prominently,
but overall,
you try to live as good a life as possible.

Fourteen existential crises a day. And that's it.
You have at least a dozen people who genuinely care.
And that's fine. This can go on for at least another thirty years.
And that's fine.

You don't have to be ravaged by every regret.
That's what assholes do.

And that's not you,
not normally,
but,
but
Tom Petty really does suck now.

When I Grow Up, March 1999

A giant juggernaut of moving quickly,
refusing to keep my hands
calm and willing to reflect patience
like lightning with a personal crusade
against some dupe with a personal relationship to god.

I just told jokes,
and I didn't feel like stopping you from treating me
like a good friend
who could have at least said something
about liking you a little bit more.

It bothered me.
Obviously and especially when you wanted me
to help you pick out an outfit
for a guy who was at least a little more masculine
than I thought I needed to be.

It shouldn't have bugged me,
but it did,
but it also didn't really get to me
to the point of the kind of trauma
that you see from people who live and breathe
and die lonely protecting their interpretation
of a shallow man's cosmic wargames.

I was almost fourteen,
so there was something to be said
for your chubby, beautiful body

flying through outfits. Your hands were so
flawless at manipulating the world
of dresses, tops, and crucial perspectives,
I stared at them as much as anything.

Your whole body was beautiful,
and I was aware of that. Of course I was.

But it was also just good to be around you.

I honestly thought we'd see each other more.

Mary Silwance

unmoored

the word sufra
is table
yet it is only when I am across the sea
from the tables I have known
that sufra reveals itself
and I discover

        like Columbusencountering a country
        without ever grasping
        it was already populated

I discover   sufra
is also   hospitality

the word sufra is   yes   a flat surface used for food
but now after all these years of eating moored at the sink
a writer who sits too much   my excuse
to refuse the table   to refuse sufra

sufra like a prism
now scatters bright
meaning through me

words unfurl into worlds
worlds unfurl into words
either and both

there are countries secreted in syllables
beyond my initial horizon
what is plain planed constrained denotation
detonates into connotation
I grasp finally table's true inhabitant
sufra is embrace

opening wide only after   do you hear me
I offer hospitality
to the scarred and scared self that navigated dark seas
that buoyed me through darknesses

when I extend sufra
to my shipwrecked self at the shore
anchor in my own harbor
in the country of my self

to feast at the table of my own making
that table at last
is sufra

because

because there is still
a blue knee on a breathless neck
because college students
are handcuffed mid-prayer
because mothers nurse
their babies as they bury them
because girls are
made mothers before they're weaned
because boys are made
soldiers while in diapers
because mining contracts
are inked in the blood of first peoples
because shareholders
make bank on bullets
because the tongues
of journalists are sliced off
because
I am a poet
and because
I am a poet
I will speak
which is to say

I will knit words

    to create a future

    our present inspires

the yarn

    I will fashion

    from every hue of the rainbow

    and more shades of melanin

    than boxes on government forms

spun

    at the table

    of together and trust and peace

    velvety as dawn

    strong as heartbeat

my needles

    one called imagination

    the other named future

imagination's metal

    formed in shorbat el yhatz

    simmering on the stove

    during this storm

    and from the early morning

    scent of Faqqua irises

future forged

    in dunes at dusk loud with birdsong

    and from the red satin ribbon sliding

    out of a cartwheeling toddler's hair

because I am a poet

    I will knit wonder

    at the harvest moon

    shimmery over olive groves

    knit gratitude for the abundance

    promised in watermelon seeds

as my needles

    root out

    centuries old splinters

    splintering each from the other

    finding places tender

    with pain and terror

I will knit home

    as wide as earth   deep as rest   soft as caress

    home   so warm you will remember

    the sun on your face as you doze in lush fields

    watching quiet clouds drift in the empty afternoon sky

    home   like encircling with your hands

    a Hebron mug   sittoo just filled with shay just for you

home

clear as a mountain stream

drenching the desert

quenching your thirst

home

breaking the wretched spell

of the razor wire hell

to reveal

all along we have been kin

all along, this is where you belong

Thank you, Menopause.

I am no longer impregnable.

meaning,   I can fuck all I want
            without   taking my temperature
                        testing my viscosity
            without   the insertion of a cooper wishbone
                        before being inserted
            without   popping daily doses
                        of pharmaceutical tic tacs
            without   being implanted
                        on the arm or ass
                        so as not to be implanted
            without   determining if my rush
                        of arousal
                        is Spongeworthy
            without   worry if a visitor
                        overstays instead of
                        leaving in a timely manner
            without   worry of breakage
                        from the cheap brand
            without   chaffing from the cheap brand
            without   worry of sabotage,
                        because erupting freely
                        feels so much better.

            Thank you,   for the pause.
            maybe now I can erupt freely

Marcus Cafagña

Beehive

Even though she's broken her vow never to do hair or nails,
never to allow her hands to wrinkle from rinsing other women's
frosted mops—let alone the wig of a one-armed mannequin,
there is nothing in her mother's life Kitty wishes to repeat,
yet, every morning, there she stands in her corner of Hairesy
Salon, bleaching another loose wave—the way in high school
she studied other women, wore her hair in a beehive like her
career counselor's—curled, teased, and sprayed into place until
the ditz advised her to forget college, said girls from the east
side of town are born to tweeze, she placing her bet on Kitty
dropping out, and now, at 42, my wife does manicures, earns
extra cash doing fingernail art for the ladies who want their
lacquer creatively cast as she sits here at our kitchen table—
painting, one by one, instead of boozing it up like her mother,
having forsaken her writing and book-reading in order to sculpt
French tips, to dab on glitter, to breathe in fumes of acetone
remover, beneath clear coats of polish, my wife—champagne
bangs falling down across her eyes—preserves whatever women
say they want to see transferred to their fingernails: miniature
heart and green high heels, puckered red lips or pink penis, erect,
until the next appointment comes.

Possession

From a beanbag on the other side of Lansing, I watch a marathon of beach flicks and fall under the spell of the television's pixilated pictures—hazy blue ocean waves that sparkle and light the dingy corners of my basement room. Distracted ogling college girls on spring break skipping through surf in their yellow polka dot bikinis, I deserve my father's remote control, because of the divorce, because one night he squeezed his fingers around my mother's throat and slammed her skull against the plaster wall. Without a job, without a TV of my own, I have taken his, missing its hum of companionship. Wallowing in the illusion of effortless movement, I closely examine the tanned skin of coeds who in real life wouldn't give a dropout like me a second glance. I stare at the screen until I feel as shallow as I imagine them to be. Six nights later, my guilt wins out. He's still out of town so I cart the Zenith back to my father's house of seven gables, use the key he doesn't know I have. With deep breaths and trembling arms, I lug the king-sized set up fifteen steps through a hallway hung with sepia-toned pictures of our relatives from the old country, drag the weighty thing banging past their disapproving faces back to its rightful place. The day my father jets home from Florida, he calls the cops, noticing the polycarbonate frame of the TV has been chipped. The reporting officer tells him something must have scared the thief away. A real pro, he figures. No sign of forced entry. My father laughs it off. Something in me wants to confess that I, his first-born son, am the thief! But when he opens the door to his house, I can hear another beach flick playing on his TV—a pleasure fest of girls gone wild over a wayward boy with blonde hair and a ukulele. When I open my mouth to speak, I can't help it. I see my father's hands again, on my mother's throat. I swallow my words, sit down beside him to watch.

Kissed a Girl

Before he slammed his fist through a wall, he screwed two nurses,
hawked health insurance, confessed he liked his women with tits
the size of hers to his boss, sold used cars, taught playwriting
in our department, kissed his student after they downed a few
in his wife's compact, behind the strip joint he suggested she
should turn into a scene before she flinched at his anecdote of the
ingénue some director humiliated by inviting his cronies to snort
lines of coke off her nipples, before he walked with a cane, before
the surgeon amputated a toe, before he lost another, before he
lost his job, friends, wife and custody of the dogs.

Jemshed Khan

Nothing Personal

nothing personal
but here we are,
sentient beings watching
ourselves watching.
powered by mitochondria,
oxygen, and sugar.
engendered by helical linkages
of paired nucleic acids,
mere byproducts
of an impersonal universe,
& I so want
to make this personal,
I want to ascribe
sacred fate or duty
to our predicament,
to my predicament,
before the molecules
of my cells and chromosomes
disperse as crematory smoke
or settle as ashes in an urn,
I see I still have time
to go Banksy on my walls.
I will stencil myself
into larger life,
tattoo quotes on my skin,
pen some wickedness,

root for the good, the bad
whatever it takes
to see myself as anything
but meaningless.

Security Screening

Terminal A
I stand
legs apart
in the plexiglass chamber,
lift my arms,
bend my elbows.
My palms rise
above my head.
Equipment whirs
and swirls
and I am
rendered naked
on the TSA screen.
A blue uniform motions me
to collect belt, shoes, wallet, and phone
from an X-rayed tray. My goods
slink back easy in my pockets
as I one-hand the belt through the loops
and make a break for the American gate.
At take-off, the buckle snugs
prim against my gut.
Turbines screech. The ground recedes.
Sunbeams tilt and joust
through twenty oval panes,
and I am on my way again.

The Shaft

I've been in this penthouse for a year. The weirdness began
in the guest bedroom: flickering lights & yo-yo window
blinds after a lightning strike. Doug from Home Automation
investigates: Bad news. Failing Lutron® processor, he says,
When those units go, a new system for a place like this runs
$50k. Notice any other unusual things?

Well... when my brother slept over he saw an apparition—
4 AM she floated by the bedroom doors, pale and semi-
transparent: drifted to the elevator door. Lights flickered and
then she disappeared into the shaft. The super says she's a
jumper from back in the 30's who haunts the place at night.
Doug laughs. I'm laughing too, but not really, because half
my brain is screaming Fifty-Fuckng-K. For that price, forget
hi-tech, I'll put my money on Ghosts.

Jose Faus

Cup Attitude

This is no Grecian urn
It has sat too long
on stacks of Borges

Its shameless in attire
See the picture
dresses up the sides
Reminds one of a pit bull
deceitful the way those eyes
entice convince you to
lower your guard before you
realize half your arm is gone

It has no handle it's proud
"Handles I don't need
no stinking handles"

I wrap my hand
struck by how well it fits
like a glove sliding easy
enveloping all the fingers
or a ring cresting the last knuckle
with a slight hitch before settling
not to budge again
The fit so secure in palm
it becomes a weapon

It's stout and cops an attitude
feels more like a tumbler
like a brawler It will
take on any other cup
It's gone a few rounds
If it were a face it would
have a broken nose
in many places
maybe an eye patch
If it spoke it would growl
menacing protective

It won't brook weak drinks
This is not a cup for tea
or two or a draw of port
it does not mind a robust coffee
prefers a half fill of mezcal
smoky hallucinogenic
preferably with fermented
pineapple juice hot sauce
and a hint of lemon zest
with a machete on the table
dust carvings in the air
from the filtered sun that
illuminates a wooden floor

It conjures up dank hovels
long nights in broken down bars
next to foggy shipyards
in lonely out of the way places
where memories have no anchors

Though It prefers to sit alone
it prowls counters looking for mates
but too picky to settle for nothing less
than Meissen Wedgewood
Royal Doulton Limoges
It once sidled up to a Ming vase
at the British museum till
it was thrown out on its lip
only to visit the next day
avec porcelain Francaise

It's a jealous cup
I'm afraid to drink from
anything else lest
I find shards in the mix

It fell once jumped right back
got into my face yelling
just cause I'm made this way
is no excuse for carelessness
you drop me one more time
and a drink will be
the last thing you'll need
so sip
sip sip
carefully

Para morir hay que vivir
(On seeing Jean Basquiat's Bird on Money)

Mad dash be-bopping
Yardbird in flight
salt peanuts salt peanuts
the first breath first mark
first step first flap first sigh

Bird on money tada
Fingers caress
a one note sustain
Dervish fingers pray
we'll see the domes of
Tunisia before light

Arrows fletched chicken scratch
teal that thing you do before blue
and black turn purple and orange
Tossed swinging ecstatic
comet burning high stepping

Para morir hay que sufrir
A green wood haze
On the way to the grave
stop create

Invasion

The pigeons bring tidings of another war
Refugee messages circle the blank-eyed cities
They would have been here sooner
but the cannonade buckled latitude
and longitude to arbitrary nodes

Unwrap the gauze lightly from the pigeon's legs
lay it flat on the table study the contours
dark edges lines the sacred text of plans
the weight of metal tracks
the metronome for melodies
of bleating trumpets

Converging planes and lines defile snow-draped fields
There is nothing new to see here or there
nothing memorializes what is readily forgotten
no monuments consecrate what was never sacred

There is no fog but a shimmering night
glimpses defining the topography of death
edicts now gray slabs and coils of iron bar
crystalized concrete in the glean of a cold moon
erased bodies fertilize the hollow ground
as a flag whips high above collapsed halls

Flags embossed on caissons pulled by mules
arrive from the cardinal directions
The sun sets again on this whirligig
You have seen them all your life

prepare your children to see them
transparent as branches in
March April and May

What is new now that yesterday wasn't full of
What will be tomorrow that was not enough today

Maria Vasquez Boyd

Cure for a love spell

When darkness came rolling over the land
Archangels cry and beat their wings

Addictive sadness is useless in the white heart of rain

I am invisible a whirling tree of air
Hair of smoke
Gold will shine through the rain

A flock of birds are summoned
then released like
love-chains on the Earth

Chinese Bells

Birds building nests
Unfinished paintings
Wind chimes in airless space

Morning coffee and cigarettes

Men she had loved
And loved her unknowingly
Now laugh

Penitent
Reserve
They slip away

Box of Fire

Two unlikely people cross paths

Bastard, she says under her breath
Whadya say? he asks

She is a box of fire
He is indelicate
He is a big clock with tiny hands, she says
She is a work of art, he says

Jeff Weddle

Rain

The day it rained
on the statue in the park
I ate an orange
and thought of roses.
The day it rained
on the statue in the park
I wrote a letter
I meant to send
but didn't.
You would have liked that day
because you loved rain and oranges
and also me, a little.
I watched it rain
on the statue in the park
eating an orange
with an unsent letter
in my pocket.
I watched it rain all afternoon
the statue and I
and the world and you
loved roses.

Burn, Baby, Burn

My daughter wants to cremate me
but I resist.
She wants to scatter my ashes
here and there.
I tell her I don't want to burn.
She laughs and says I'll be dead
and won't be able to do anything about it.
My wife chimes in, wondering why
I would deny our daughter this pleasure,
as if it's the most normal thing in the world
to suddenly decide to be cremated
on the whim of a child.
My daughter also likes to go to bookstores,
just the two of us,
to ride shotgun for hours
listening to each other's music,
to intensely discuss writers
I'm certain her friends
and even her teachers
don't know.
She bakes cakes and cookies for the family
and takes beautiful, tiny Polaroid pictures
with a camera she got two years ago
at Christmas.
We watch too much TV together
and she wants to cremate me.
She laughs and says she'd be happy
to do it while I'm still alive.
My daughter is a lot of fun
and I'm pretty sure she loves me,
so I decide she's joking.
I think that's for the best.

Blocked

I was once certain I had lived
a novel
but that wasn't so.
The girl, the highway, the ocean.
The screams and regret.
The lost night and wandering
until, by chance, I find my friends
drinking in some tourist bar.
The sex and the double cross.
The whispers and laughter in the dark.
All the years after.
I was once certain
about a good many things.
Now, I'm down to this:
Nothing lasts.
Nothing comes true.
Also, I don't know where any of them
are now, neither the living, nor the girl,
nor the dead.

Kyle Laws

Every August

The pale blue of sky
                means water is near
a river along which deer travel early

a time of day when all that's possible
                lies in front of you as you look up
and stare into the distance.

I've sat for years in a small room
                at the top of stairs and wrote
into a cantaloupe-colored morning

about what is grown in fields east
                in Rocky Ford and La Junta
as I headed to Kansas on Highway 50.

If the Painting Were an Abstract Woman

Her mother sews next to the pot-bellied stove
providing not heat, but atmosphere for dining.
Together with the room next to it, the bar stood
here when this was Fagin's Saloon.

In spring, we walk through waves of seabirds
too tired to be fearful. Famished from flights
from South America, the birds fuel on horseshoe
crab eggs while the sea rushes in onto sand.

After counting the number of men at the table
three times, I decide twelve is too many. It looks
cluttered even though it's the number of eggs
in a carton.

There is basketball at St. Raymond's gym for girls
on Wednesday and Friday dances at St. Barnabas
by the Bay where the daughter throws Catholic
foul shots and dances to Episcopal soul.

In this abstraction, blood of a prehistoric creature
smears red when in fact it is blue, something we
learn from sticks poked through its hunched shell.
A vaccine for coronavirus may be harvested here.

Fence Line

a painting by Diana LaMorris

An arrow to trees at the foot of Pikes Peak
purple as only Katherine Lee Bates' poem
that I reminded myself to sing on the 4th
of July. I told this to an Episcopal priest.

She said how close we were to where Bates
went in a wagon to the top and we bonded
as two would when one's from Boston
and the other Philadelphia.

Me, born the year my family bought a bar
on the Delaware Bay in New Jersey
upstairs rooms converted to an apartment
to make the mortgage payments.

This where the right whales once ran and
the original settlers found it too bitter year-
round so moved upriver with Penn to what
became Philadelphia. Now what's celebrated:

the running of shorebirds from South America
to the Artic for summer, South Jersey where
they stop to feed on eggs of horseshoe crabs
laid in the sand May to early June.

Melissa Fite Johnson

Sylvia Plath in the Kitchen, Matthew Perry in the Jacuzzi

His last Instagram post, purple moonlight, so relaxed
in the place where he'll die a few days later, this picture
a time capsule. He doesn't know, the way none of us know,

all our death dates uncircled. They slink by every year,
like shadows, like tumors. Forgive me,
I've been rewatching *Friends,* which is not

how Matthew Perry wanted to be remembered,
but I didn't know him, I only knew Chandler,
I only knew Esther, Pecola Breedlove, Holden Caulfield,

Dylan McKay. Forgive me, I'm an English teacher.
And a 90s kid obsessed with TV. Whatever,
no distinction, no high or low brow. They're all stories.

They're all characters. Today a student said
we judge Janie Crawford because she doesn't exist
and I felt like crying. They all exist, more than any of us—

next semester I'll introduce him to Elizabeth Bennet
and Jane Austen's been dead over 200 years.
Her only authenticated photo a painting her sister made.

Ode to the Royal Rumble

Sure, everyone starts pointing all dramatically
at the Wrestlemania sign in January,
months before Wrestlemania,
you can get to thinking Wrestlemania

is the point, but what kicks off Wrestlemania
every January? The Royal Rumble,
superior in every way,
a parade of elaborate entrances

and bravado, every 90 seconds
a new countdown that the crowd chants,
that you chant at home,
don't act like you don't, and then

that terrible buzzer that shocks
even though you know it's coming,
though you don't know who's coming,
not until the first seconds

of a theme song, and sometimes
it's a letdown, AJ Styles, technically
excellent but uninspired, or Brock Lesnar,
clearing the ring without heart—

but sometimes it's Kofi Kingston,
who you know will fly from the ring

but handstand his way back in,
he should win every year but never has,

and sometimes it's Edge,
emerging in a haze of smoke,
glorious return after the neck injury
kept him away nine years. Literal fireworks.

A man in the crowd
squeezed his eyes shut and thanked
his God. My husband and I cried.
Edge cried. You cried, too—don't act like you didn't.

High School Was Nothing Like
Sweet Valley Promised

Probably, I never would have tried cocaine anyway,
but sweet deaf Regina Morrow doing it once at a party
and dying sealed it (*On the Edge*, Book 40).

I was such an Elizabeth in high school,
and not Elizabeth after the motorcycle wreck,
amnesia-wild with Bruce Patman (*Dear Sister*, Book 7),

the regular Elizabeth, dependable and naïve and good old,
terms guys dismissed me with before spotting my friends
the Jessicas at parties. Not cocaine parties, God no,

like themed parties, like dances, like prom
where Jessica spiked Elizabeth's drink
so Jessica would win prom queen, of course

Elizabeth got drunk from three sips and drove, of course
Jessica's boyfriend Sam died (*A Night to Remember*,
Book 95). OK, not like that either,

I was such an Elizabeth but for real, no morality play,
no manufactured drama, I never had a boyfriend
or smoked pot, I thought this meant I wasn't wild,

no one would ever want me. Blame Francine Pascal
for killing Regina and Sam, killing innocence,
blame her for all the boys loving Jessica,

for Bruce Patman (again!) cheating on Regina

which drove her to the cocaine party

in the first place—but who can I blame for the rest of it.

DeAni Blake-Britton

Blessed Are Those

Catering to nature's habits,
God's hand grips a palette knife
and spreads tawny jam between terracotta buildings
from a jar labeled: THE FRESH DEATH OF SPRING AND
    SUMMER.
His ten acolytes spend a couple months
plucking the scene, then play
a contemplative melody along the keys
of hallowed paintbrush handles.

He plunges one into water and wipes the slate clean.

Now, the world is sandwiched between two pieces of snow:
one toasted, the other a gigantic huff of still smoke.
In un-spackled corners, he draws pines shelved with white,
and messy nests where hushing branches upend dormant birds.
Behind a railing, a woman stares into a wrinkled blue
mouth that gurgles a spoiled gutter's milk.

Tomorrow, out of boredom, God will make the world a runny
nose.
Cars will slide their sticky wheels along highways,
balding trees will sluff off the rest of their pin cherries,
and the woman wondering why nothing belongs to itself
will be smudged into the gaping, toothless blue.

Wider Than The Wound

you tore the earth open

                                        by word of mouth
                                        made it a wound
                                        without sound

someone there called my name

                                        again +
                                        again +
                                        again

there was something like red moss

                                        rusted windows painted shut
                                        mosquitoes resined
                                        between stained glass

a stalemate in the kitchen sink

                                        cruelty in the cabinets

a Radio Flyer and a double-leg cast

                                        a mother pulling her
                                        child across the cavity
                                        their open mouths

calling me
wider than the wound
without sound

Late-Night Walk

We shivered through sleek streets
and showers of rusted leaves,
past warm-white heads on slim-black bodies
and bronze statues darkened by autumnal night.
Funny how you won't recall a thing.

We passed rows of eroding shrubbery
where hot pink chrysanthemums once blossomed.
Their rigid and sickly green petals
smell like nothing now—
a nothing you'll forget by the end of tonight.

We passed burrowed Cottontails, wild strands
of spider webs, and the lulling creek
littered with cicadas, toads, and ghostwood.
Everything is unfragranced by fall.
Funny how you won't recall a thing.

Clarence Wolfshohl

The Church of the Holy 33½

Movement 1

He lifts the disc above eyes
into the realm of light
glints off the polished
surfaces. He squints at the edge
of the disc's thousand cosmic orbits
inscribed decreasingly toward the hole,
the center to wrap around
the chromatic chromium spindle,
the unmovable prime mover. Not a speck
of dust, not a smudge
of finger, not a scratch
of needle; it is
immaculate and ready to conceive
heavenly melodies as the rhythm
of the spheres da-da-dums
into the bodies of true believers.

Movement 2

The disc now held at its edges
between prayerful palms, fingers splayed
so not to violate the platter's
surface, is lowered in swaying
genuflection onto the stereophonic
altar. The stylus is raised,
the disc revolves around

the unmovable prime moving spindle,
electricity begins the cosmic hum.

And as stylus touches
softly vinyl eucharist, CRACKLE ....
then deep throb of cosmos
dum dum dum   dum dum dedum dum
bass and organ set the line
all must abide. Heavenly harp
choogles off the walls, and the atomic guitar
explodes mushrooms of visions
in the inner eye of they who worship . . .
Wow, man, wow!

Movement 3

It is passed around
holy weed of sacrament
one toke over every line
as the communicant
drops from knee
to knee with tender
words and touches
some sway
and crescendo
with the cosmic jam
others sit cross-legged
in navel contemplation
or recline in the arms
of blessed mother ROCK . . .
Far out!

Nectar

fritillaries bounce
        on the air
               around me

        nearly daring
to light and sip

        the sweat off my brow

as I weed
        the garden three feet
               from the milkweed patch

purple blooms   bear up
hundreds of butterflies
        in that ten by ten jungle

               a lone sweat bee
        safaris through
        my arm hair
               to siphon off
the nectar of my sweat

his cousins of several species
share the milkweed pollen
               and nectar
with the butterflies.

Fishing in Early Spring

Two horses graze the fenceline
behind me. One is a mare, chestnut;
the other, hardly a horse, more
pony, also chestnut. I can hear
their chomping, the grass tearing loose,
occasionally a swish of tail
at whatever April bug is dancing
before them. The mare blows
what sounds like a raspberry,
perhaps a comment on my lack
of luck along the shoreline next to their fence.

A sweetness from whatever is blooming
up the slope rolls down to me. I search
and besides the pointillist redbuds
near the summit, all I see are the poles
and guidewires and seasonally pruned
grapevines someone refreshes his spirits by.
The wind is at my back as I cast
once more. It chases the water
from the edge of this pond
into choppy wavelets under which moss
is tossed to and fro, up and down,
like the air dancers in front of car dealerships.
The fish are in there, too smart to bite
and enjoying the neighborhood of horses

Andrés Rodríguez

The Magi

Every year I see them cross those wastelands
by night, no moon, no clouds, only stars
roaming above a land in bondage, unrest
drifting on the wind. In their brown faces,
I think I see the loss of one of their own,
and doubt about to make them turn back.
Yet in those old and graceful features,
I see dreams too, even of their companion,
not lost but standing on Athena's Hill,
absorbing radiant night. It pushes them on.

With all their strength they move forth,
always the one star that harnessed
their pilgrimage working in them
with its will and brightest light.
That king who summons them
makes their souls turn to gall,
so they promise him anything:
their desire not to conciliate men,
but to proceed toward the great object,
to carry what they bear in their hands.

When they arrive, they see no palace,
no court of kings or summoned slaves,
only a rocky, treeless town surrounding
a depth of space, a fold within night's cloth
surrounding a different kind of star,
a tear emerging at the rim of an eye
that each of them sees as his own.

Love pierces them. Or it's the madness
that comes with exhaustion, hunger,
loneliness and fear which makes their

essence melt out into that cave
where a man, woman, and child
fill the dark with a faint breath of music.
In their looks there is no finer love
that brings the pilgrim home,
that carves out a nest of the deepest
darkest brightness. That new flesh,
Child of Stars, is a gift to old men
fallen on swollen knees who find
something old and new growing in them
before turning home to face the future.

To the Girl in the Belger
Art Gallery (Who Took My
Picture on the Hottest
Day of the Year)

July's supercharged heat
burns everything, even
chars the air. I wander
with the others through
the vault of images,
better than the movies,
weightless as dreams,
needing only the candor
and mystery of the eye.
Then behind me a voice
swims past the pictures
to dive on my nerves.
I turn to see her there
stepped down from a picture,
her hair's straight black
part of the gallery dark,
her flesh filling a dress
as currents fill
a body of water they're made of.
Where her dress ends,
thighs glow foam-white,
shadows flowing around them.
Poised below her eyes,
at the center of my vision,
she holds up a camera.
"Do you mind?"

The question deafens me.
My soul wants capture,
my soul resists capture,
here among seen spirits
residing in this nocturne,
this hidden pageant
safe from winds outside.
But in these hushed rooms,
before doubles of us
in sweet or agonized poses,
love's habits or griefs
pull me into beguiling fire.

Before I can hear again,
the dark puts a gleam
in her nose stud,
the same brief, casual light
of a moment's gift or need.
Dreaming or second waking,
hostage to some unerring
desire or hoped-for chance,
I stare, rapt not by what I see,
but by the callous voice
that doesn't wait for chance.
"I just want your picture,"
she says and pulls the trigger,
not waiting for a yes or no.
Beauty gets what it wants.
A single flash pounces.
She has the photo.
I have the image.

The Groundhog

Humbly, like the new prairie grass
stippling the earth, like the pink
dawn rivering the sky, he arrives
rising from currents below earth
that flow through hidden rooms
shining in the dark. This emergence
rivals the triumph of wing on wind.

Who could gas or blast him?
Let him dwell in our grey spaces,
where he stops falling ashes
with a look as he gobbles grass.
And that whistling engine
signaling danger before he disappears
to womb warmth deep below
streams through the dying elm trees
and the single peregrine in the air.

His home is silent perfection.
Think complex spaces of the small,
protected from town-leveling winds.
Not the feel of solitude,
but a place inside a place for
dreaming, nursing, feasting, growing.
That nest beneath us,
the first cradle we emerged from
before we broke open the sky,
before we stood on two feet rising
above the horizon without reason—

he never left that kingdom,
singing in his dark garden.

I wait for a dawn or afternoon
to see his footprints in the mud
or catch a rare glimpse in a tree,
roly-poly devotee risking a few berries
high above the littered ground.
He risks life itself in this city,
crossing streets where steel nightmares
flatten everything in their path,
or burrowing under houses,
a pest to those who kill not for

self-preservation but because it's easy.
To those in their domain of rush and rage,
a groundhog is just a brown paper bag
at the curb, crumbled, stained black.
I would take "trash animal" from their lips,
take gross certainty from their minds,
and show them the spiral thread of life
woven in the earth, the precise
and furtive and traceless dream
they should see and possess.

But I can only make what I can.
Several yards behind the house,
in a stand of trees that release light
generously in every season,
there is a garden just for one.
Carrots, turnips, lettuce, sweet kale
rise and fall and rise again

as he waddles into view each day
to eat and grow fat and live another day
in this imperfect made heaven.

Huascar Medina

Monody For Citians In Urban Decay

unlike folded paper floating downstream in the shape of voyages
atop urban runoffs we're not destined to fall into gutters or storm
drains pull us up before the downpour floods the sidewalk full
of strangers walking hand in hand with dreams humming in their
lungs some of us can't swim through concrete cities drowning
on stone stranded on gray there were kinder places before
gentrification where sunlight did not have to work so hard to
climb above a skyline to bring us this kind of morning where air
and breathing dissonate

Captain America eats cake on the 4th of July

Today is not your birthday Steve but if you're invited to a
patriotic party offer to blow out the red, white & blue sparkling
candles screaming like fuses.

Make a wish on behalf of Old Glory so it isn't replaced with an
Appeal to Heaven so we can make it to a quarter millennium.
Try to make America better. That would be super.

Found Transcript: *Typewritten by the Wind on the Heads of Triticum Aestivum**

We are bountiful, said the Horizon to the Skyline. We are rising, emerging ahead, growing upright like rows of grain-filled wheat.

Every act of breaking bread begins here, in these fields—where you and I meet. Right here, in Kansas, where souls are weighed in bundles, not grams.

* Bread Wheat

Alison Erazmus

Unconscious

I used to think
the unconscious is a fascinating place
Freud & revolutions & the structural theory of the psyche
a vast dark plain I do not control
where anything can happen

I was not yet rocked by night terrors
jolting me into daylight
afterwards they sit in consciousness
like mercury in the liver

these feelings and thoughts swing tree to tree
on neurons and synapses the lights go on and on

a thousand neurons told me this violent thought
a thousand neurons gave me this traumatic memory on a Tuesday
at work

Now I think
my mind is such cruel place
the horror film
the dark hallway
covered in blood
I walk towards a strange sound

In this mindset
the yoga teacher says to breathe
the sponsor says to breathe

the meditation app says to breathe
the internet says to breathe

in
out

to stop my avalanche
or to ride it

here's what also might help

a mother's reassurance and monologues about family members
    dying
a warm bath while reading self help books
a campfire to burn personal effects
a cat laying across your shoulder

these are my hands of mercy

what's yours?

Renters

I had four oracles
All different and mostly useless

I came to them for guidance
Each recommended I take a walk

One finally told me
what my dream meant

'You are fixing up a place
you do not own.'

She reminded me:
I had a house
I had a home
I had a husband
I had a life

Her dreadlocks and her coffee skin
She spoke some truth

I am the fixing type
I fix things that don't ask for it

Building utopias
Picking up the tools
Left by other Figures
Much bolder than I

The dream reappears
After a day of planning & chiseling & sanding

Slowly, slowly
I carve
My name
I show
My hand

Brought to light
The dream reminds me of when
I am fixing up a House
I do not own

Years from now
Will people curse my
meddling?

Or will they revel
In my wild work
Hammers hammering

Am I a gnat?
Or am I an ant?

I say
We are all renters

Some of us paint
A fresh coat on walls
We do not own

Even though we understand
We will never own a thing

Church

My Sunday church
begins at 5600 feet above sea level
Sunrise service!
The runners we pass all say
'Good morning'

Good morning to you!
A prayer of goodwill
to my fellow trekker
Sun beams during sunrise
strong as a spotlight but fills the sky

You bow your head
Ooo ah
Bless this earth
We worship and sing
We take notes during sermon

Then down the steps
towards another world called heaven on earth
Near creeks
People prattle and sing
Hallelujah
Hallelujah

Communion at the canteen
and the mule
How did humans ever make such a place?
in this church of the canyon

Baptisms in the river
Shale like stained glass
People are holy
Our bodies are divine
But pain happens too
This is life

On the way out
We tell each other 'I believe in you
Yes you can, you're almost there'
Life is mostly uphill and
'Do you need help?'

The fellowship we felt in the struggle
on mud and packed ice
pressure on the chest

Rest houses to
rest your weary heart and legs
Then rise and go

To the summit
Where I turned the corner
and started to cry
at the sight of the arch
Made with million year old rocks
Sea shells and human determination

We did it!
This heavenly body
attending my Sunday church

Justin Hamm

HEROES   EAT NOTHING

ravens

feast   on

Thought and Memory

a poet

upon men as well as   the gods

-from Edith Hamilton's *Mythology*

IN THICK SMOKE

Mother Earth

could bear no more

all on fire

the flames

a   pity   so bold

upon the tomb

the Sun God s

mourn

the   end of

the story

-from Edith Hamilton's *Mythology*

A LONELY GIRL

        in a copper boat

fashions a long rope

      of the   moon

    but   she does not open

her eyes

           ever

-from "The Process of Individuation," M. L. von Franz.
Man and His Symbols edited by Carl G. Jung

William Sheldon

Fruitless

In the raking light of a western sun,
the flowering crab, a Thunder Child, rests
just outside the shadow of the damaged
Bradford Pear, a third taken by the ice
that turned out our lights for six days.
We cooked soup on the wood stove,
read by candles, and showered
at the Y.
　　　　　　　Smoke from the pear's logs rise
from the stove sometimes on winter days.
July now,
the bank sign claims 102.
The Labrador, drags a maple limb fallen
over the fence from the neighbor's yard.
Her predecessor's ashes mix in the garden soil
where our tomatoes fail to redden. Flies
hang on the screens signaling a storm,
and the hen, foot hurt by a hail stone, hops
to the font. The sun drops below the line
of cottonwoods. A fingernail moon rises in the east.

Just A Moment

A rose in the rain, a bowl of fruit.
A man with a guitar
begins to play. A candle lit,
a box unpacked, a book put down.
Clouds pass across the moon;
the dog stirs in her sleep. Through
the open window, air rich with onions,
shivers the flame. The song strays
to a minor key. A woman's hand
rests on the guitarist's shoulder.
He smells onions. The dog,
awake now, barks, hackles raised.

Like Jarry's

—though   fueled by less
alcohol, and no ether—
his dreams had come
to seem alive as days.
Nights spent behind
the wheel of his dreams,
driving towns he'd known,
strange now, roads
longer, exchanges
leading places familiar
and unknown, a poem
without a map.
The ethereal clung
to his waking.
His home, opposites,
with other plans,
new rooms appeared,
and women,
known and not.
A central stair, no walls
led to a loft, double bed,
light always morning.
Traveling a street
traversed some twenty years,
he might look left
not knowing which house
or store front would arise,
wake mourning
some curtailed chance,

open a door in his own
home uncertain
of the room behind
or who reclined
on what couch.

The Players

Walter Bargen has published 27 books of poetry including: *My Other Mother's Red Mercedes* (Lamar University Press, 2018), *Until Next Time* (Singing Bone Press, 2019), *Pole Dancing in the Night Club of God* (Red Mountain Press, 2020), *You Wounded Miracle*, (Liliom Verlag, 2021), *Too Late to Turn Back* (Singing Bone Press, 2023), and *Radiation Diary: Return to the Sea* (Lamar University Press, 2023). He was appointed the first poet laureate of Missouri (2008-2009). His awards include: a National Endowment for the Arts Fellowship, Chester H. Jones Foundation Award, and the William Rockhill Nelson Award. He currently lives outside Ashland, Missouri, with his wife and too many formerly feral cats.

DeAni Blake-Britton is a Californian living in Missouri. She's a recent college graduate, Sigma Tau Delta alumna, mango enthusiast, and burgeoning poet.

Maria Vasquez Boyd is producer/host, of Artspeak Radio a weekly live program on 90.1FM KKFI Kansas City Community Radio. Since 2012, she features local and world renowned artists, writers, poets, playwrights locally and internationally. Boyd is a founding member of the Latino Writers Collective, a storyteller, poet, artist, designer, painter, and continues to exhibit her work across the country. She served as Poet in Residence for *Present Magazine* in Kansas City, Missouri.

Tony Brewer is a poet and audio artist from Bloomington, where he is executive director of the Spoken Word Stage at the 4th Street Festival of the Arts and Crafts and co-producer of the Writers Guild Spoken Word Series and the Urban Deer Performance Series. He has published 12 books and chapbooks, including most recently Centaur (with Jonathan S Baker, Dark Heart Press) and Good Job, Lightning (Stubborn Mule Press).

Steven Bridgens Born: Kansas City, Missouri, August 17, 1949 Died: Kansas City, Kansas, January 31, 2017 Resurrected: that very same day, in fine shape. Current Fascinations: words, poems made of words, paintings, assemblage, the rearranging of the Ten Thousand Things, sculpture & the mystery of the empty plinth, the ancient world or the idea of it, silence & its absence, sleep & the same, dead bluesmen & women, the artist & the muse, dead gods & the demimonde, the primeval forest of Buddhism in its humble glory, the savage tyranny of the political stage, the toxic & enlightening proscenium of the internet, the Jungian depths of the self & the unconscious, the flickering shadows of cinema & architecture, the utopian possibilities of life on Garden Earth with our fellow passengers, all beings finally liberated.

Steve Brisendine lives, works and remains unbeaten against The New York Times crossword in Mission, KS. He is the author of five collections of poetry, most recently *full of old books and silence* (Alien Buddha Press, 2024) and *Behind the Wall Cloud of Sleep* (Spartan Press, 2024). His work has appeared in Modern *Haiku, I-70 Review, Flint Hills Review* and other publications and compilations. He has no degrees, one tattoo and a deep and unironic fondness for strip-mall Chinese restaurants. In his spare time, he tries to make himself seem far more interesting than he actually is.

Marcus Cafagña is the author of three books of poetry, The *Broken World,* a National Poetry Series selection, *Roman Fever,* and *All the Rage in the Afterlife This Season.* His poems have also appeared in *Ploughshares, Poetry, Rattle, Southern Review, Springfield News-Leader,* and *Out Here, We Say "Mizzoura!": An Anthology of Mizzoura Poetry.* He serves as professor emeritus of poetry at Missouri State University.

Beverly Cartwright is a writer currently residing in Richmond, VA. She is at work on her first collection of poetry as well as a memoir. Her work has been previously published in *Oddball Magazine, Raven's Perch* and *Stone Poetry Journal.*

Lesley Day is the author of the poetry collections *Authenticity, The Absence of Light,* and her forthcoming collection, *IMPACT – A Woman's Story from Surviving to Living* from Ink Soul Publishing. Day has been published in several anthologies and online magazines. She resides in a small town in Missouri, where she raises her two sassy daughters and one silly pupkid.

A native of Los Angeles, **Chase Dimock** lives in a four-person household, including a human partner, a Cavalier King Charles Spaniel companion, and a four-foot tall statue of Slimer from Ghostbusters. He serves as the Managing Editor of *As It Ought To Be Magazine,* holds a PhD in Comparative Literature from the University of Illinois and makes his living teaching literature and writing. His debut book of poetry, *Sentinel Species,* came out in 2020 from Stubborn Mule Press.

L. Dopa is a former truck driver and professional wrestler who now lives in a trailer park in Big Tuna, TX where he writes poetry, looks at the stars and is also a passionate HAMM radio enthusiast. He may be reached at luchadorpress@gmail.com or at instagram.com/l._dopa/.

Alison Erazmus is a visual artist and writer originally from the agricultural landscape of northern Illinois. She is currently based in Saint Louis, Missouri. She earned a Master of Fine Arts degree with an emphasis in photography from Southern Illinois University Carbondale in 2008. Until recently, most of her creative practice entailed making photographs (sometimes paintings) but more and more poems came to her in 2022 so she started writing them down. While working as a curator she has self-published curatorial essays for visual art exhibitions she developed, mostly of photography, prints, and textile art. Writing about visual art in an accessible way for many readers and audiences helped her develop as a writer overall. In 2024, her poems were in Angels on a Sylvan Road, produced by Myrtlehaus Publishing. She currently works in animal welfare, so a lot of her poems are about taking care of cats.

José Faus is a writer, performer and visual artist. He is a founder of the Latino Writers Collective and sits on the boards of The Latino Writers Collective and Charlotte Street Foundation. His writing appears in numerous anthologies. His chapbook This *Town Like That* was released by Spartan Press. His second book of poetry *The Life and Times of Jose Calderon* was published by West 39 Press.

Linzi Garcia can be found frolicking through fields, cemeteries, bookstores, and bars across the states. Her full-length poetry collection, *Thank You,* was published in 2018 by Spartan Press, and her chapbook about studying abroad in London, *Live a Great Story* (co-written with Jase Buck), was published by Analog Submission Press (2019). While getting her MA in English at Emporia State University, Linzi worked as the graduate assistant to Poet Laureate Emeritus of Kansas Kevin Rabas and as an editorial assistant with Bluestem Press and *Flint Hills Review.* Linzi now serves as the publicist at Meadowlark Press and the poetry editor for its imprint, Meadowlark Poetry Press.

Transplanted from Western New York, **Ken Gierke** has lived in Missouri since 2012. His love for nature, fostered by the Niagara River, continues in Missouri and is often featured in his poetry. His writing has appeared as two micro-chapbooks from Origami Poems Project. His poetry is part of an anthology edited by d. ellis phelps, as well as in collections by the *Gasconade Review* and the Columbia Writers Guild, and has been featured by numerous online journals. His poetry collections, *Glass Awash* in 2022 and *Heron Spirit* in 2024, were published by Spartan Press. Hiswebsite: https://rivrvlogr.com/

Poems by **Alex Gildzen** have appeared in a coloring book, a dozen anthologies, at least a hundred magazines and a bench in downtown Palm Springs. A multiple Pushcart Prize nominee, he has won the President's Medal at Kent State University and an Ohioana Award. He has edited *Dress: Journal of the Costume Society of America* and co-edited *A Gathering of Poets*. Gildzen's photographs have appeared in *Plain Dealer Sunday Magazine* and *New York Times Style Magazine* as well as book covers for NiteBallet Press, Crisis Chronicles Press and Poems-for-All. He was featured in the documentary "Big Joy" and has been an extra in mainstream films and a supporting player in independent films. He has been a model, with and without clothes, for painters and photographers.

Pilar Graham is the author of *Currents* (2022). *Falling*, her second collection of poetry, is forthcoming summer 2024 with Stubborn Mule Press. Her poetry has appeared in Cold River Press - *Voices Anthology; Sundog*, Haunted Waters Press; *Indent Literary Journal;* Finishing Line Press; *Blackberry*, among others. Publications for her creative nonfiction essays include *Essay Daily; The Broiler: A Journal of New Literature; Poetry Midwest;* and *Pithead Chapel Press*. Graham has served as a literary editor and judge for local and national writing competitions. Graham earned her MFA in Poetry from California State University, Fresno and teaches at California State University, Monterey Bay, and part-time at Fresno City College. Graham is currently seeking publication for her third collection of poems, *Forever, Becomes,* in addition to a collection of creative nonfiction essays, *Burn Scars,* www.pilargraham.com.

Beth Gulley is a Kansas City based poet who has published three chapbooks and four full-length collections of poetry. Her most recent books include *Dragon Eggs* (Spartan) *Picking Fights in Book Club* (Bottlecap Editions) and *Frog Joy* (Anamcara). Beth serves on the Riverfront Reading Committee and the Writers Place board. Most people recognize her from her coffee addiction and messy hair. More information can be found on her blog at https://timeeasesallthings.wordpress.com/.

Originally from the flatlands of central Illinois, **Justin Hamm** now lives near Twain territory in Missouri. He is the author of four books of poetry, *Drinking Guinness With the Dead: Poems 2007-2021, The Inheritance, American Ephemeral,* and *Lessons in Ruin,* and a book of photographs entitled Midwestern. He is also the creator of Poet Baseball Cards and the founding editor of the museum of americana.

Caitlin Johnson is the author of three chapbooks and two full-length poetry collections, including *Delta* from Stubborn Mule Press. Her work has appeared in *Pembroke Magazine, Vagina: The Zine, Slippery Elm Literary Journal,* and many others. She lives in Michigan.

Melissa Fite Johnson is the author of three full-length collections, most recently *Midlife Abecedarian* (Riot in Your Throat, 2024). Her poems have appeared in *Ploughshares, Pleiades, HAD, Whale Road Review, SWWIM,* and elsewhere. Melissa, a high school English teacher, is a poetry editor for *The Weight,* a journal for high school students, and *Porcupine Lit,* a journal by and for teachers. She and her husband live with their dogs in Lawrence, KS, where she co-hosts the Volta reading series at the Replay Lounge.

Mike Jurkovic's poetry, prose and music reviews have been published globally but with little reputable income. Full length collections include: *Buckshot Reckoning*, (Luchador Press 2023) *mooncussers*, (Luchador Press, 2022); *AmericanMental*, (Luchador Press 2020); *Blue Fan Whirring*, (Nirala Press, 2018); Anthologies include: *Calling All Poets 25th Anniversary Anthology* and *CAPS 2020* (CAPS Press); The Shape of a Curve (GWFM, 2023); *Reflecting Pool: Poets & the Creative Process* (Codhill Press, 2018); *Like Light: 25 Years of Poetry & Prose* (Bright Hill Press, 2018); *WaterWrites: A Hudson River Anthology*, and *Riverine: Anthology of Hudson Valley Writers* (Codhill Press, 2009, 2007) A 2016 Pushcart nominee, he is President of Calling All Poets, now in its 25th year in the Hudson Valley. He serves as co-chair of the Music Fan Film Series, Rosendale Theatre, Rosendale, NY. CD reviews appear online at All About Jazz and lightwoodpress.com Featured poet: London, San Francisco, NYC, Albany, Baltimore, Philadelphia. Host, NuJazzXcursions, WVKR 91.3. FM Vassar College. *Chronogram*, 2003-2006. *Elmore Magazine*, 2009 - 2014; *The Van Wyck Gazette*, 2013 - 2020. *The Rock n Roll Curmudgeon* appeared in *Rhythm and News Magazine*, 1996-2003.

J. Khan is based in the midwestern US and has published in diverse magazines including *Coal City Review, Chiron, SPRR, I-70 Review, Rigorous, Unlikely Stories, Fifth Estate, Writers Resist, Barzakh, and shufPoetry*. In 2021 his activist chapbook *Speech in an Age of Certainty* was released by Finishing Line Press. He is completing a full-length book that narrates the underworld adventures of the Maya Hero Twins as an illustrated epic poem.

Julianne King is a poet, essayist, and bibliophile living in Pacific, Missouri. King's poetry collections include *Bible Belt Revolution, Sex Work & Other Sins, Honeysuckle, Hanging Art*, and her upcoming collection *Dandelion Love*.

Nancy Krieg does not feel like a victim, though she believes one should write from experience. She lives in NKC and works at a popular Hawaiian restaurant. While her job is taking money she insists it is "looking for a joke". Her collection of poems entitled *Cool Shades of Eventide* is available from Spartan Press.

Lynne Jensen Lampe's debut collection, *Talk Smack to a Hurricane* (Ice Floe Press, 2022), a 2023 Eric Hoffer Book Award winner and finalist for the 8th Annual McMath Book Award, concerns motherhood and mental illness. Her poems appear in journals such as *The Inflectionist Review, Journal of Compressed Creative Arts,* and *THRUSH* as well as anthologies in the US, UK, and Germany. She edits academic writing, reads for *Tinderbox Poetry Journal,* and lives with her husband and two dogs in Columbia, MO. https://lynnejensenlampe.com or https://linktr.ee/lynnejensenlampe for socials.

Kyle Laws is based out of Steel City Art Works in Pueblo, CO where she has a studio-gallery and directs the Pueblo Poetry Project. Her collections include *Alchemy of Rooms* (Osage Arts Community Press, 2024), *Beginning at the Stone Corner* (River Dog, 2022), *The Sea Is Woman* (Moonstone Press, 2021), *Uncorseted* (Kung Fu Treachery Press, 2020), *Ride the Pink Horse* (Stubborn Mule Press, 2019), *Faces of Fishing Creek* (Middle Creek Publishing, 2018), and *Wildwood* (Lummox Press, 2014). With nine nominations for a Pushcart Prize and Best of the Net, her poems and essays have appeared in magazines and anthologies in the U.S., Canada, and Europe. She is the editor and publisher of Casa de Cinco Hermanas Press.

Gary Lechliter's work has appeared in many poetry journals and anthologies. He has published five books of poetry and one chapbook. His most recent book *The Silence of Wrens* was published by Woodley Memorial Press.

Dawne Leiker is a former journalist and native of western Kansas. She is the author of two collections of poetry, including *Death of the Civic Minded Man* (self-published) and *what remains* (Spartan Press, 2022). Her work has appeared in Coffin Bell, Moving Force Journal, Liquid Imagination, and other publications.

A professor emerita of Bethany College, **Linda M. Lewis** has been an activist, critic, editor, actor, educator, mother, and grandmother. She is the author of numerous essays and four scholarly books on British and world literature (University of Missouri Press). Recently she published two books of poetry, *Ensemble* (2019) and *This Swirling Largesse* (2022)—both by Spartan Press. She lives, writes, and gardens in Lindsborg, Kansas.

R. Nikolas Macioci earned a PhD from The Ohio State University, OCTELA, the Ohio Council of Teachers of English, named him the best secondary English teacher in the state of Ohio. He is the author of nineteen books. *Cafes of Childhood* was submitted for the Pulitzer Prize in 1992. In 2021, he was nominated for a Pushcart Prize and a Best of the Net award. In 2022, he was nominated for a Pushcart Prize. He was nominated for a Best of the Net award for 2023, and *City of Hammers* was nominated for a Pulitzer Prize. Hundreds of his poems have been published here and abroad in magazines and journals, including *Chiron Review, Concho River Review, The Bombay Review, The Raven's Perch, The Main Street Rag,* and *West Trade Review.* He won First Place in the 1987 National Writer's Union Poetry Competition, judged by Denise Levertov, First Place in The Baudelaire Award Competition, sponsored by The World Order of Narrative and Formalist Poets (1989), Second Place in *Zone 3's* first annual Rainmaker Awards, judged by Howard Nemerov (1989), Second Place in the *Writer's Digest* annual competition, judged by Diane Wakoski (1991), and he received the Blaine R. Hall Award for best poem of the year in *Kentucky Poetry Review* (1991).

Kansas Poet Laureate emeritus (2019-2022) and Academy of American Poets Laureate Fellow, **Huascar Medina** has authored two books of poetry: *Un Mango Grows in Kansas* and *How to Hang the Moon*. He is the Lit editor for seveneightfive magazine, a staff editor at *South Broadway Press* in Denver, CO, an op-ed writer at *Kansas Reflector,* a founding member and former Chair of TopekaUnited.org, the founder of wordssavelives.org, and co-founder of latinidad.us. Huascar works for Mid-America Arts Alliance as an Artist INC program associate, providing professional development programming to artists over a six-state region. He is President of Artsconnect Topeka's Board of Directors, a Kansas Book Festival Advisory Committee Member, a Salina Spring Poetry Series Curator, a member of the Accessible Arts Greater Kansas City (AAGKC) Roundtable, and a National Council on the Arts Member.

Al Ortolani's poetry has appeared in journals such as *Rattle, New York Quarterly*, and *Prairie Schooner.* His most recent collections are *The Taco Boat,* published by New York Quarterly Books in 2022, and *Swimming Shelter* from Spartan Press which was named a Kansas Notable Book for 2021. His novel *Bull in the Ring* was released by Meadowlark Books in 2023. He is a winner of the Rattle Chapbook Prize and has been featured in Garrison Keillor's Writer's Almanac and Ted Kooser's American Life in Poetry. Ortolani recently directed a memoir writing project for Vietnam veterans in association with the Library of Congress and Humanities Kansas. As a retired high school teacher, he enjoys a life without bells and fire drills. He's a sucker for auctions and garage sales. Ortolani is a husband, father, and grandfather, currently entertaining the idea of becoming a hermit. However, his wife prefers the company of the neighborhood feminists, and his dog Stanley refuses to live without treats.

Michael Poage was born in Virginia. He has published fifteen books of poetry, most recently, WHY THE WILL TO PUNISH?, Spartan Press, 2023. He served as the Poet-in-Residence at Dzemal Bijedic University in Mostar, Bosnia & Herzegovina, 2018, and has taught English literature and ESL courses in Latvia and, virtually, in Thailand as well as in Bosnia and Herzegovina. He lives in Wichita, Kansas with his wife, the historian, teacher, and activist, Dr. Gretchen Eick.

Matthew Porubsky is a writer born and raised in Topeka, Kansas. He is the author of voyeur poems, *Fire Mobile* (the pregnancy sonnets), *John, Ruled by Pluto*, and *Serpent's Lap*. He currently works as a copywriter at the University of Kansas.

Past Poet Laureate of Kansas (2017-2019) **Kevin Rabas** teaches at Emporia State University, where he leads the poetry, playwriting, and filmmaking tracks. He is a seventh generation Kansan. He has sixteen books, including *Lisa's Flying Electric Piano*, a Kansas Notable Book and Nelson Poetry Book Award winner. He is the recipient of the Emporia State President's and Liberal Arts & Sciences Awards for Research and Creativity, and he is the winner of the Langston Hughes Award for Poetry. His plays and films have shown across the Midwest and on both coasts.

Gabriel Ricard writes, edits, and occasionally acts. He writes a monthly film column called *Captain Canada's Movie Rodeo* at Drunk Monkeys, as well as another monthly film column called *Make the Case* with Cultured Vultures. In addition to his columns and books of poetry, fiction, and essays, he is also a writer and performer with Belligerent Prom Queen Productions, perpetually working on a follow-up to their 2016 immersive theater show Starman Homecoming. His horror movie podcast *The Hounds of Horror,* co-hosted with an actual man from Florida named Chris Bryant, is available everywhere. This insatiable, aging weirdo has traveled tens of thousands of miles on Greyhound, failed at standup comedy, worked in radio, performed at haunted houses all over Long Island and New Jersey, and still can't remember to close the shower curtain. Gabriel currently lives in Orlando, FL with his wife, crazed ferrets, someone else's dog, a few billion teddy bears, and a crushing inability to stop ordering delivery.

Kevin Ridgeway's books include *Too Young to Know* (Stubborn Mule Press) and *Invasion of the Shadow People* (Luchador Press). His work has appeared in *New York Quarterly, Hiram Poetry Review, Gargoyle Magazine, Paterson Literary Review, Slipstream, Chiron Review, Nerve Cowboy, San Pedro River Review* and *Trailer Park Quarterly,* among others. He lives and writes in Long Beach, CA.

Andrés Rodríguez is the author of *Portal of Dreams* (Woodley Press) and *Night Song* (Tia Chucha Press), both poetry collections. He is also the author of *Book of the Heart* (Lindisfarne Press), a study of the letters and poetics of John Keats. He is a recipient of a Maureen Egan Writers Exchange Award in poetry from Poets & Writers. He has twice been nominated for a Pushcart Prize in poetry. His poems have appeared in *Blue Mesa Review, The Cortland Review, Drunken Boat, Harvard Review, New York Quarterly, Valparaiso Poetry Review,* and other literary journals. His degrees in English are from the University of Iowa, Stanford, and the University of California.

Alexej Savreux is a poet, satirist, and art and music journalist. His books include *Graffiti on the Window, Eat Me & Other Short Poems, Asoak in the Knight's Moat, The Ballad of Lady Vigilance,* and the chapbooks *the arithmetic of the heart* and *Blue Coffee*. Additionally, Alexej has authored or co-authored other works, including *The Neo-Expressionist Mathematica* and a variety of unfinished screenplays and cookbooks. A second-generation Czech-American born in Burlington, Vermont, he has spent most of his life in Colorado, Kansas, and Missouri. He has received grants from the University of Kansas, The NEA, and The Charlotte Street Foundation. Alexej is a proud Step Up Community Learning Center graduate and was a visiting artist at the Kansas City Art Institute in 2023. He lives in Kansas City, Missouri, where he works odd jobs. He is a frequent contributor to KC Studio and previously served as a Special Correspondent for The Kansas City Star.

Tyler Robert Sheldon's seven poetry collection include *Everything is Ghosts* (Finishing Line Press, September 2024) and *When to Ask for Rain* (Spartan, 2021). He is Editor-in-Chief of *MockingHeart Review* and Assistant Managing Editor of *Dialogue: The Interdisciplinary Journal of Pop Culture and Pedagogy,* and his work has appeared in *Last Stanza Poetry Journal, The Los Angeles Review, Pleiades, Quiddity, Tinderbox Poetry Journal,* and other places. His research interests include poetry and poetics, comics studies, pedagogy, and World War II. A Pushcart Prize nominee and winner of the Charles E. Walton Essay Award, Sheldon earned his PhD at LSU and his MFA at McNeese State University.. He lives in Baton Rouge, where he teaches, writes, and usually has a cat on his lap. View his work at TylerRobertSheldon.com.

William Sheldon is the author of four collections of poetry, including *Deadman* (Spartan Press). *When I Go West: New and Selected Poem*s is forthcoming from Meadowlark Press. He plays bass for the bands The Excuses and STOP.

Scott Silsbe was born in Detroit. He now lives in Wilkinsburg, Pennsylvania. His poems have been collected in four books: *Unattended Fire, The River Underneath the City, Muskrat Friday Dinner,* and *Meet Me Where We Survive.* He is also an editor at Low Ghost Press.

Mary Silwance lives in Kansas City and is a mother of three daughters. She teaches adult EAL, is a KCAI writing adjunct, and facilitates workshops on writing as well as ecology for area organizations. Mary serves on the editorial teams of Whispering Prairie Press and Flying Ketchup Press, where, as Poetry-Editor-in-Residence, she conceptualized and was editor of, *Of Our Own Accord,* an anthology of women's embodied experiences released in 2024. Mary published her first full-length collection of poetry, *We Remember Ourselves,* also in 2024. You can find her publications, radio, and zoom presentations as well as workshop offerings on writing and ecology at https://www.marysilwance.com. Mary's work focuses on the intertwining of personal and collective emancipation to create a lush future for all beings.

Sharon SingingMoon is a poet and award-winning visual artist living in mid-Missouri. She draws inspiration from the natural world and our human struggle to balance mind/body/spirit in the face of our own hubris. Sharon has a Master's degree in Public Administration and worked as a lobbyist for social justice issues, spearheading several progressive advancements in Missouri before retiring. She now hosts a monthly Reading Series, SPOKEN, and was co-editor for *Rough-Cut Elegies An Anthology of Missouri Poets* 2024 (Spartan Press). Sharon's work has been published in *Anti-Heroin Chic, Masticadores USA, Spillwords, Silver Birch Press, To Light the Trails, Sidhe Press, Interpretation*s, several volumes of *Well Versed* anthology and others. Her poetry collections, *The Weight of One Hummingbird Feather* (Spartan Press) and *Random Seed* (Compass Flower Press) can be found at independent bookshops across the mid-west as well as Barnes & Nobel and Amazon.

Richard Stimac has published a poetry book *Bricolage* (Spartan Press), two poetry chapbooks, and one flash fiction chapbook. In his work, Richard explores time and memory through the landscape and humanscape of the St. Louis region.

Timothy Tarkelly's work has appeared in *Calf Magazine, Unstamatic, Clayjar Review*, and others. He has authored several collections of poetry, including *A Horse Called Victory* (Kelsay Books), *The You We Know and Love* (Spartan Press), and *Angie and Her Roommate* (Alien Buddha Press). When he's not writing, he teaches and coaches debate in Southeast Kansas.

William Trowbridge's tenth poetry collection, *Father and Son*, was published by Wayne State College Press Press in April. He is a faculty mentor in the University of Nebraska-Omaha Low-residency MFA in Writing Program and was Poet Laureate of Missouri from 2012 to 2016. For more information, see his website, williamtrowbridge.net.

JD Vail is a poet living in Columbia, Missouri and the author of three poetry chapbooks so far and the creator of the "I Write Books With JD Vail" podcast. JD completed the MFA in Writing program at Lindenwood University in 2011.

Maryfrances Wagner's newest books are *The Immigrants' New Camera*, and *Solving for X*. She co-edits *I-70 Review*, serves on The Writers Place board, was 2020 Missouri Individual Artist of the Year, and was Missouri's 6th Poet Laureate 2021-2023. *Red Silk* won the Thorpe Menn book award and was first runner up in the Eric Hoffer award 2024 (reissued in 2023) and Short Listed for the Grand Prize. Poems have appeared in *New Letters, Midwest Quarterly, Laurel Review, American Journal of Poetry, Poetry East, Voices in Italian Americana, Main Street Rag, Rattle, Unsettling America: An Anthology of Contemporary Multicultural Poetry* (Penguin), *Literature Across Cultures* (Pearson/Longman), et. al. She is the granddaughter of four Italian Immigrants.

Jeff Weddle, the State of Alabama Beat Poet Laureate, is the author of 16 books, including the Eudora Welty Prize winning *Bohemian New Orleans: The Story of the Outsider and Loujon Press* (University Press of Mississippi, 2007). His most recent book is a poetry collection, *Driving the Lost Highway* (Uncollected Press, 2023). A new collection, *A Letter to Xhevdet Bajraj*, is forthcoming from Uncollected Press, with an expanded version also forthcoming in Albanian translation in Kosovo, which will be his second book in translation with Publishing House SabaiumBB. Jeff teaches in the School of Library and Information Studies at the University of Alabama.

Clarence Wolfshohl is professor emeritus at William Woods University. He has been active in the small press as writer and publisher for over fifty years, publishing poetry and non-fiction in many journals, both print and online, including *New Texas, San Pedro River Review, Agave, Cape Rock,* and *New Letters*. Among his publications are the e-chapbook *Scattering Ashes* (Virtual Artists Collective, 2016), the chapbook *Holy Toledo* (El Grito del Lobo Press, 2017), *Queries and Wonderments* (El Grito del Lobo Press, 2017), and *Armadillos & Groundhogs* in late 2019.

Nettie Zan lives and works on art and meditation in the great watershed state of Missouri. Residing at the intersection of science and spirit, Zan creates visual, written and experiential art. They are currently working on "the small gods of animals," a primitivist investigation of our shared humanity. They are an artist in residence at InterUrban ArtHouse and you can find out more at nettiezan.com or follow @listenmore .

This project was made possible, in part, by generous support from the Osage Arts Community.

Osage Arts Community provides temporary time, space and support for the creation of new artistic works in a retreat format, serving creative people of all kinds — visual artists, composers, poets, fiction and nonfiction writers. Located on a 152-acre farm in an isolated rural mountainside setting in Central Missouri and bordered by ¾ of a mile of the Gasconade River, OAC provides residencies to those working alone, as well as welcoming collaborative teams, offering living space and workspace in a country environment to emerging and mid-career artists. For more information, visit us at www.osageac.org

Osage Arts Community